RANCIÈRE'S SENTIMENTS

RANCIÈRE'S

SENTIMENTS

DAVIDE PANAGIA

DUKE UNIVERSITY PRESS

Durham and London

2018

Text designed by Matthew Tauch
Typeset in Arno by Tseng Information Systems, Inc.

Library of Congress Cataloging-in-Publication Data
Names: Panagia, Davide, [date] author.
Title: Rancière's Sentiments / Davide Panagia.
Description: Durham : Duke University Press, 2018. |
Includes bibliographical references and index. | Description
based on print version record and CIP data provided by
publisher; resource not viewed.
Identifiers: LCCN 2017031014 (print)
LCCN 2017044092 (ebook)
ISBN 9780822372165 (ebook)
ISBN 9780822370130 (hardcover : alk. paper)
ISBN 9780822370222 (pbk. : alk. paper)
Subjects: LCSH: Rancière, Jacques—Criticism and
interpretation. | Rancière, Jacques—Aesthetics. | Rancière,
Jacques—Political and social views.
Classification: LCC B2430.R274 (ebook) | LCC B2430.R274
P363 2018 (print) | DDC 320.01—dc23
LC record available at https://lccn.loc.gov/2017031014

Cover art: Photo of Jacques Rancière by Lea Crespi /
LUZphoto/Redux.

CONTENTS

THE MOTIVATIONS that bring one's attention to an author's modes of handling words, vistas, and dispositions are many. Literary and theoretical interests are hardly specifiable topics but rather a spectrum of sensibilities and affinities. In the case of reading Jacques Rancière's oeuvre, the matter of literary and theoretical interest is even more complicated. I encountered Rancière's work for the first time in 1993, as I was completing a master's thesis on theories of ideology, and as I proceeded to develop my interest in his writings I felt the need to cultivate a series of strategies and repositionings of my readerly expectations so as to deal with what I felt were persistent displacements. Simply put, I never felt that Rancière's corpus offered a theory of judgment, and at the time I believed a theoretical interest demanded the elaboration of criteria of judgment so that I could assess the nature of political and aesthetic value. How does Rancière judge the works he engages? Why does he judge them in that way? And how does he articulate the priority of judgment for politics? Not only did his writings not provide me with a theory of judgment, but they didn't even provide me with a reason as to why judgment matters. And that seemed incredibly disorienting: How is it that an author so committed to thinking the relation of aesthetics and politics doesn't divine a method of judgment, or even celebrate judgment as a political faculty?

The most controversial aspect of this book on Rancière's aesthetics and politics is my claim that Rancière is not a theorist of political judgment, that he does not defend a theory of judgment as crucial to political life, and that his intellectual ambitions are not committed to elaborating interpretive methods for understanding the meaning of aesthetic works or a hermeneutic system for the political interpretation of artistic objects. This isn't to say that he makes no judgments of his own, nor that he doesn't provide assessments for things like works of art or political events. But Rancière has no interest in articulating political practices as somehow enabled or emboldened by capacities for making judgments — reflective, determinative, or otherwise.

Instead his project is to articulate new forms of criticism that look to the workings of things. "The critic," he says, "is no longer a person who compares a work to a norm and says if it's well done or not. . . . The critic is the person who identifies what's happening."[1] And this, for him, means "constructing the sensible world to which the artwork belongs or which a political act makes possible."[2] This ambition for criticism puts him at odds with a substantial strain of Anglo-American political theory devoted to the celebration of judgment's freedom potential, whether that strain is identified with a defense of Kantian reflective judgment, as is evident with the Arendtian tradition of theorizing judgment, or is the parallel tradition that situates the power of the imagination as the source and site of continuity and innovation for the development of political ideas in the North Atlantic and Mediterranean territories, as is exemplified in the work of Sheldon Wolin.[3] And, finally, this puts him decidedly at variance with those normative theories of political judgment committed to the application of a concept, a norm, or a criterion for the assessment of the success or failure of an action.

This is not the same as saying that Rancière's political and aesthetic ambitions are to take the possibility of making judgments away from individual or collective actors. On the contrary, for Rancière politics comes with no qualifications — even the qualifying condition that individuals and collectivities ought to be capable of making judgments. It is to say, then, that for Rancière the elaboration or assertion of theories of judgments is not where politics happens. This is because the pronouncement of a judgment already presumes a system of criteria for participation in the scene of judgment's locution that, in the end, always appeals to the faculty of understanding. Simply put, an appeal to the politics of judgment is an appeal to comprehension, to a specific form of intelligence, that some may have and others won't: it is an appeal to self-reflexivity as an account of knowing and perceiving the world, an appeal that stands as a qualification for political participation. And for Rancière, such an intellectual qualification breeds inequality. This is no doubt aided by the fact that in French the expression *le bon sens* is used to designate the good sense, the agreeable sense, and common sense all at the same time. The linguistic conflation here projects the point that the pronouncement of a judgment will, in the end, always be regulative in some way.

Hence the centrality of scenes of "disagreement" in Rancière's work, which, as I elaborate in the pages of this book, do not stage a dispute between competing understandings but rather stage *mis*understandings — or better, they are scenes of *missed* understandings: a talking at crossed purposes, if you will, where there is no sense that interlocutionary coordination is a goal or even an ambition. One might say, in this regard, that Rancière is a thinker of incommensurability in the dictionary definition of the term ("having no common standard of measurement; not comparable in respect of magnitude or value")[4] and that for him any and all forms of judgment are normative precisely because they demand our signing on to a prepolitical commitment to understanding that betrays a specific way of orienting one's self to the world, a partition of the sensible.

Though this articulation of Rancière's stance on judgment may seem surprising given that we are dealing with a thinker who has opened up an entire field for the study of aesthetics and politics, it shouldn't be. Rancière's intellectual and political career is punctuated by repeated instances of standing up to judgment's authority — not just, that is, to the authority of judgments but to the normative stature of the concept of judgment in political life. We see this in Rancière's published critiques of Althusser's scientism, but we also see it in his own life as an activist and autodidact, where experiences have shaped his commitment to what he will call the ignorant method.[5] Biography and individual experience here matter because, as we know, Rancière's intellectual work emerges from and is entangled with his personal history of political activism, his experiences studying in a highly segmented university system, his autodidacticism, and his having participated in a series of political movements ultimately judged unsuccessful.[6] Many of the ambitions that motivated an entire generation of students and scholars of the 1960s and 1970s were thwarted despite furtive engagement and political activity, not to mention literary and intellectual productivity. The result was a subsequent series of denouncements that judged those political activities as unadulterated failures. What to do, then, with the fact that the task of judgment (regardless of its genre and mode of elaboration) is to identify and denounce political failures? What to do with the accusation of political failure and the subsequent dismissal and denunciation of one's political ideals? Rancière's answer is to treat the scene of critical judgment as radically insufficient and inegalitarian.

Rancière thus privileges the activity of partaking (i.e., *partager*) over the activity of judging. Partaking is his site for the exploration of an ecology of dispositions, sensibilities, and forms of participation by individuals, groups, objects, and histories who have been repeatedly judged as unentitled to participate because their assigned mode of acting in the world does not include the specific activity in question — whether that might be writing, filmmaking, political theorizing, or grassroots organizing. Given this, no amount of discussion, justification, elaboration, or validation will suffice to legitimate those agents in their forms of participation. This is because whatever reasons they might give, the simple fact of their doing what they are doing — the simple fact of their participation in an activity — is improper. This, at its core, is the formal scene repeatedly staged in Rancière's writings, and it is a scene that can't be addressed or resolved by an appeal to theories of political and aesthetic judgment.

In short, what distances Rancière from judgment-oriented political theory is his view that the game of validation is actually a retroactive description of a multitude of happenings occurring at one time and that it is unwarranted — from his perspective — to consider the plethora of activities in any space and time as either reducible or beholden to the expectations of responsiveness, as if politics happens because something like persuasion or reason-giving or acknowledgment is available to action. Rancière's actors don't have that sense of responsibility to responsiveness. They are part-takers. They act by taking part in an activity that doesn't belong to them and that they have not been tasked to do.[7] And they don't spend their time making or justifying arguments to one another, or to others, because their doings are improper and any reason they may give for their actions is de facto illegitimate.

I am reminded at this point of a passage from Linda Zerilli's *Feminism and the Abyss of Freedom*, where she offers one of the most astute and compelling accounts of the politics of judgment. Placing Rancière alongside Cavell and Arendt, she affirms, "Aesthetic and political judgments, in which there is no concept to be applied, raise the question of criteria in an acute way, for saying what counts involves something other than the activity of subsumption. Unique to such judgments is that the subject does not recall the grounds upon which things can be rightly judged, but is called upon to elicit, in relation to specific interlocutors, the criteria appropriate to the particular at hand."[8] Like Arendt (via Cavell), Zerilli wants to extend Kant's claim (articulated in the *Critique of Judgment*) that aesthetic experience solicits a sense of freedom and that that sense of freedom arises from the experience of ungroundedness that emerges from one's encounter with an object of taste. The absence of a concept that might be applied to that particular moment of experience with an object raises the possibility of a criteria-less condition of coexistence between individuals.[9] The result for Zerilli is a calling upon the subject of experience to be responsive to the experience by eliciting criteria that acknowledge the moment of ungroundedness. And this "being called upon to elicit criteria" is an important dimension of politics and — especially — of freedom.

No scenario could be further from Rancière's orbit of thinking about aesthetics and politics. This, for several reasons. The first is that for Rancière, politics isn't about being called upon to elicit criteria for counting; it is about the *making* count, regardless of whether or not that activity is persuasive to others. The condition of inequality — which is his basic starting point — is such that the giving of an account is pointless. Try as you might, if your voice is deemed noise, then any account you can give simply won't count. In other words, Rancière is especially diffident of the dynamic whereby we are called upon to account for our experiences, our criteria, ourselves. This is because the language game in that scene of hailing already presupposes a set of conditions that individuals might have in common — most notably the fact that sounds coming out of my mouth are words rather than blabber, that providing criteria is a relevant fact about political behavior, that it is decorous to give reasons to others, that we must be responsive to one another in that way, and that we are capable of hearing the call of responsiveness and accountability. Second, Rancière's political actor is not a subject (of language, of judgment, of experience, etc.). Participation in activities produces the possibility of the emergence of a particular coordination of subjectivity. But there is no subject that exists prior to participation in an activity.

Further to this, the hailing scenario implies a schema of power that assumes a specific form of intelligence as a qualification for participation. It doesn't matter, then, whether you think of judgment as the application of a concept that proves one's argument or whether you describe it as an activity of being "able to say how one came to an opinion, and for what reasons one formed it."[10] In either instance, what is being proscribed or required is a qualification of intelligibility of and for the world. On the judgment model, what precedes politics is an already agreed-upon commitment to the authority of responsiveness that compels one to have to provide reasons about one's forms of perceptibility and sensibility. In short, the problem for Rancière is pedagogical: theories of judgment presuppose a prepolitical authority that qualifies the dividing line of political participation. This goes directly counter to his "method of the ignorant" that he describes as "the opposite of the method that first provides a set of general determinations that function as causes and then illustrates the effects of these causes through a certain number of concrete cases. In the scene, the conditions are immanent to their being executed. This also means that the scene . . . is fundamentally anti-hierarchical. It's the 'object' that teaches us how to talk about it, how to deal with it."[11] The challenge of Rancière's writings is to engage a scenographic critical disposition committed to the arrangement and rearrangement of participatory forms instead of, or in the place of, a critical method that elaborates reasons for judgment and the conditions for their implementation.[12] His is a sensibility that attends to the specific arrangements of a situation and their reconfigurations so as to surmise not so much a radical political program that might be followed as the absolute limits of an occurrence such that politics is incipient.[13]

To appreciate this sentiment is to begin to see how compelling and unsettling an aesthetics of politics can be for political thinking. The ambition of this book is to tease out the distensions of such unmoorings.

ACKNOWLEDGMENTS

I HAVE BEEN STUDYING the writings of Jacques Rancière since graduate school. As a result I have accrued more occasions of acknowledgment than I care to (or even can) remember — acknowledgment of interlocutors, of critics, of those who dismissed the ideas and those who embraced them; acknowledgments of learning institutions, publications, and other spaces that have accommodated my interventions; and acknowledgments of texts, writings, resources, and works that have inspired or thwarted my own ideas. These are the acknowledgments of a life of learning wherein any gesture of responsiveness will inevitably seem like a contrivance. I have, where possible, tried to detail those debts in the text itself.

Some specific individuals come to mind. As I was completing my PhD, Bruno Bosteels invited me to Cambridge, Massachusetts, to meet Rancière, who was visiting his department at the time. A belated thank you to Bruno! Out of that first meeting many other events emerged, including copublications with Rancière, conferences, and the like. But really, a friendship. And so, of course, I must thank Rancière for the times we have been able to share in various cities, from Cambridge to Baltimore, Milan, Paris, Peterborough, and LA. And I must also thank Danielle Rancière for the hospitality she shows me when I visit them in Paris.

As the reader will note, the work of Frances Ferguson creeps in throughout this book. Her work is central to my thinking about aesthetics, formalism, and politics, and I have benefited from an intellectual camaraderie with Frances for many years. For this I am truly grateful.

I wish to acknowledge all the students who have taken classes with me and have engaged my willingness to consider aesthetics and politics as conceivable together, who have worked through the syllabi I cobbled together, and who have pushed me in their own writings to consider other possible arrangements. Thank you, then, to Katharine Wolfe, Jo Anne Colson, Adrienne Richard, Liam Cole Young, Troy Bordun, Duane Rousselle, Matthew Hamilton, Summer Renault-Steele, Dilyana Mincheva, Duncan Stuart, Cody Trojan, Alex Diones, Anna Scheidt, John Branstetter, and Jared Loggins. I owe a debt to the institutional spaces where I have taught and that have given me more or less free rein to teach what I thought best. In this the Cultural Studies Department, the Center for the Study of Theory, Culture, and Politics, and the Politics Department at Trent University and the Department of Political Science at UCLA are exemplary.

Lisanna Gussoni, my partner in life and all that is wonderful, took time, made time, and indulged my anxieties of needing time so that I might spend just one more minute with my computer screen. That I can dedicate myself to writing while raising a family is thanks to her understanding, love, strength, and above all patience.

A substantially altered section of chapter 1 appeared as "Partage du sensible" in *Rancière: Key Concepts*, edited by Jean-Philippe Deranty (Durham, UK: Acumen Press, 2010). Chapter 3 originally appeared as "Rancière's Style" in *Novel: A Forum on Fiction* 47, no. 2 (2014): 284–300. Part of the discussion of Nouvelle Vague cinema in chapter 2 appeared as "Show, Don't Tell" in *Politics, Theory, and Film: Critical Encounters with Lars Von Trier*, edited by Bonnie Honig and Lori J. Marso (Oxford: Oxford University Press, 2016). The kernel of chapter 4 appeared as a book review in *Critical Inquiry* 41, no. 2 (2015): 464–65. I thank these venues and their editors for permission to reproduce elements of those works here.

Once again a sincere debt of gratitude goes to Courtney Berger at Duke University Press, who was enthusiastic about the manuscript in its early stages and chose the two most intelligent and encouraging reviewers I could have requested for this project. Also at Duke, Sandra Korn's stewardship throughout the publishing process was attentive, responsive, and invaluable. Pushing me in all the right ways, these people's curatorship of this project was transformative.

At a late point in the revision process one of the Duke reviewers revealed themselves to me. That person is Lori Marso, with whom I've been in conversation and critical exchange for many years. Lori pressed me in her inimitable way to make explicit what I thought obvious in the manuscript, and she invested much time and effort (beyond the traditional labors of a reviewer) in encouraging me to write the best work I could write. But more than this, even before this project ever began, Lori took me to task about my formalism, pressing my ideas and formulations, my commitments and sensibilities. In short, she made me appreciate the possibility of articulating a formalist aesthetics vis-à-vis a radical democratic political imaginary. And for that I am forever in her debt.

I dedicate this book to my mother, Maria Luisa Vercellotti, whose courageous choices in life taught me of the risks that came with traversing the dividing lines of immigration—back and forth, and back again—but also what hopes and opportunities await. She took it upon herself to provide my brother and me with a sentimental education, teaching us the value of persons, objects, places, and spaces that mesmerized. Those experiences stuck, but what really stuck was the importance of those experiences to my life.

INTRODUCTION

The Manner of Impropriety

THIS BOOK is about Jacques Rancière's aesthetics and politics. It distinguishes itself from other works on or about Rancière's thought by giving emphasis to the simultaneity of aesthetics and politics in his oeuvre and to his styles of reading, writing, and thinking.[1] I am less committed to the application of his ideas than I am to describing the distensions and extensions of his literary operations. One of the central contentions of this book, then, is that stylistic arrangements matter to Rancière's aesthetic and political thought. I thus pay heed to his scenographic mode, which "consists in choosing a singularity whose conditions of possibility one tries to reconstitute by exploring all the networks of signification that weave around it."[2]

Throughout these pages I explore the networks of sensibilities that weave in and through Rancière's writings. Hence the title, *Rancière's Sentiments*. A central tenet in my recounting of Rancière's intellectual enterprise is that he is best considered a sentimental thinker and author, by which I mean he is the kind of thinker who believes that one's sensibilities and perceptibilities play a leading role in one's disposition to the world and to others, and that the work of politics is the work of arranging and adapting, if not transforming altogether, world-making sensibilities and perceptibilities. Hence the simultaneity of aesthetics and politics and his scenographic mode of reading, writing, and thinking.

The idea of scenographic arrangements and sentimental dispositions have political corollaries, namely solidarity, emancipation, equality, and participation. Rancière's aesthetics and politics address emergent collective formations that arise from the active participation of individuals and groups unauthorized to partake in those same activities that constitute their collectivity. The objects and persons he recounts in his books are all objects or persons who are not authorized to express sentiments, sensibilities, and actions but who nonetheless realign affective practices of time and space, of systems of value, and partake in the work of expressivity. The result is a transformational scenario of the conditions of participation and of how we think solidarity, emancipation, and equality. Such transformations are conceivable as akin to the ways artistic explorations of the limits of specific media imply not just a new instance of that medium but an entirely new medium. Thus with Rancière it's not just that the occupations he describes in any particular scene imply a new way of participating in solidarity or emancipation or equality; more radically such reconfigurations imply new forms of solidarity or emancipation or equality. In short, Rancière's aesthetics and politics offer us an affective pragmatics for a politics of equality and emancipation.[3]

The most readily familiar example of the transformative happenings of improper partakings is that of the worker-poets in nineteenth-century France whom Rancière recounts in *Proletarian Nights* and who took time at night to write rather than sleep. Such acts of literary production generated a series of disruptions to the extant regimes of sensibility, not the least of which is a realignment of the temporal regime that dictates who is and who is not entitled to leisure. Through their aesthetic activities the worker-poets "took back the time that was refused them by educating their perceptions and their thought in order to free themselves in the very exercise of everyday work, or by winning from nightly rest the time to discuss, write, compose verses, or develop philosophies."[4] These discrete forms of improper participation disrupted the circadian rhythms of labor's day. Through their acts of literarity, the nineteenth-century worker-poets quite literally *took time* they didn't have; theirs was an act of reappropriation of a propriety not assigned to them. They created a new medium of dayness, not simply a new instance of it. The result is a rearrangement of a series of sensibilities and perceptibilities that generate a novel mode of solidarity of persons, places, times, and practices—a new staging, if you will, or a new partition of the sensible.

Politics for Rancière thus begins with an act of aesthetic impropriety, with a refiguring of the line that separates the sensible and the insensible. For him everything has the same potential power of sensorial appearance: anything whatsoever can appear or speak or sound. For this reason no partition between visible and invisible, audible and inaudible, is a necessary quality of the object or scene in question. Perceptibility is a condition of arrangement in the way that comprehension is a matter of composition. To be sure, lines of division do exist. But these lines are not natural objects in the world. And the work of emancipation and equality involves the aesthetic rearrangement of lines that, through discreet activities of tinkering, attests to their malleability.

Much of my exploration of Rancière's aesthetics and politics focuses on repeated moments in his writings that aim to put on display how aesthetic practices that transform perception and sensibility are also political practices of emancipation, solidarity, and participation, and vice versa. For what carries weight in these instances of aesthetic and political simultaneity is the capacity to arrange relations, and therefore worlds, anew regardless of one's assigned ways of being and doing. I consider such approaches characteristic of sensibility thinkers (from Francis Hutcheson and David Hume to Jane Austen, Laurence Sterne, and Gustave Flaubert, to William James, Walter Benjamin and Gilles Deleuze) who place less emphasis on specific accounts of the meaning of things (whether events, texts, or symbols) and focus instead on the centripetal and centrifugal forces that enable persons, places, and things to relate.[5] Rather than the affirmation of political concepts that require an unpacking of their propositional content, then, terms like *emancipation, solidarity*, and *participation* are—from a sentimental point of view—relational forms that dispose and arrange bodies and create frictions and fluidities for the transformation of existing arrangements.[6]

More to the point, I show the extent to which, for Rancière, these practices of transformation don't simply point us to new sources for thinking about traditional concepts of solidarity, equality, or emancipation. That is, it's not simply the case that Rancière is suggesting we can arrive at these concepts from more directions than we have hitherto imagined. It is the case that, given his own explorations of specific scenes of arrangement and rearrangement, these ideas are markedly different: each scene of solidarity bespeaks a new experience of a 'becoming with.' Notably Rancière will emphasize the pragmatic dimension of these activities. Solidarity, emancipation, and equality aren't concepts, in other words; they're practices. And if we consider them practices, then each iteration of the practice is unique precisely because every scene manifests a specific configuration of forces and objects and persons. That is to say, the construction and reconstruction of the sensible world to which a specific activity and event of assembly-forming belongs means that we can't speak of a general concept of solidarity or equality or emancipation. This is a fundamental point about aesthetic experience: it is born of the particular (not the general) and is resistant to the general application of a concept. Hence there are no general concepts of solidarity, emancipation, or equality. There are only scenes whose "conditions are immanent to their being executed."[7]

Such formulations, and such ambitions, mark one of the reasons Rancière has frustrated many commentators (Peter Hallward is best among these) who can't find in his oeuvre an instrumental rationality (or *praxis*) for political action,[8] while others attempt to devise supplements to his insights by articulating a theory of responsiveness as a complement to his provocations. In this respect Aletta Norval's ambition to cultivate an ethos of aversive responsiveness that is neither presupposed nor predetermined in the scene, but emergent from it, is exemplary. "This includes, crucially," she affirms, "an emphasis not only on the perspective of the articulators of a wrong, but on their addressee, those occupying privileged positions within the extant order. It requires attention to historical specificity and singularity, just as it calls for an emphasis on the politics of claim-making and the fragile collectives it brings into being."[9] Now while such political ambitions are admirable extensions of Rancière's work, and the theoretical sophistication of Norval's position is limpid, the ambition here is still to demand some form of redemption beyond the imminence of the scene — an aspirational teleology that, as we shall see (especially in chapter 2), is denied by Rancière's critique of the structure of authority in Aristotelian poetics. The most challenging fact about Rancière's work is that through his mode of reading and writing — that is, the sentimental disposition evident in his arrangement of words, ideas, events, and objects on a page — the reader is compelled to have to come to terms with a radically alternate sensibility of what political thinking is. Or, better, what it is not: for Rancière, political thinking is not in the business of producing "advice to princes" literature. His way of doing political thinking is not committed to the prescription of concepts, ideas, and norms for the purpose of a political program.

Rancière's Sentiments thus enacts what I call a sentimental readerly mood in order to access the networked distributions of juxtapositions, allusions, and assertions that occupy his writings.[10] Allow me, then, to say something about the status of the sentimental in my approach to reading and in my descriptions of Rancière's project. I follow James Chandler's account of the sentimental and its proximity to the Roman rhetorical sense of *dispositio*, a term that refers to the arrangement, assembly, or indeed disposition of things — of the ordered arrangement of individual parts into a composite whole. "The sentimental revolution in literature that dates from the mid-eighteenth century is not just about new kinds and levels of feeling but also about ways of ordering works and organizing the worlds represented in them," Chandler explains.[11] A sentimental mood is what Rancière invokes and deploys when affirming that politics is about the reconfiguration of the sensible fabric of an existing order.[12] The decorum attributed to a given way of sensing, or a common sense, would be one such arrangement. And so when Rancière names his political actant "the part of those who have no-part,"[13] he is naming an amorphous force that is at once immanent to but also extraneous to decorum. The no-parts are un-arranged and un-arrangeable according to existing dispositional regimes; they are not agreeable, to use a belletristic term of art. Politics for Rancière happens when the extant norms of how things fit can neither sustain nor explain the existence of discrete parts that don't fit. Such fragments don't account for an exclusion so much as an inability to register a relation with an established sense of ordering. Thus what is required is the articulation of a new disposition, arrangement, or networks of sensibilities. Such acts of rearticulation are what Rancière calls *partager*, and they are acts that refer to moments of radical mediation where the inequalities of qualification that enable access to politics are rendered indistinct.[14] Anyone can partager anything whatsoever, to rework Jacotot's famous precept that "everything is in everything."[15]

One of Rancière's most compelling formulations of this aesthetic and political entanglement is when he speaks of "the measurelessness of the mélange" so as to register an amorphous form of solidarity devoid of any common principle that might act as a qualifying condition for participation in the ensemble.[16] As we will see, he is troubled by the term *commons* and its coupling in recent democratic theory with a capacity for consensus as the necessary qualification for participation in democratic life. That is, Rancière is troubled by the tendency in recent democratic thought to reduce the commons (*le commun*) to the in-common.[17] The expectation of having to sign on to a common set of conditions in order to belong to and thus participate in various forms of political action is at the heart of consensus theories of democratic representation. At their most basic such accounts of political participation demand capacities like judgment and attention of their agents and presume that a capacity for judgment or a specific mode of attention (and thus a particular account of intelligence) is necessary for politics. But Rancière's formulation aims to affirm an immanent and amorphous political form that resists fitting into the available schema of accountability; it affirms that there is always more stuff in any coordination of time and space that any institutionalized form of counting can accommodate. Precisely because anything can make a sound or appear, the specification of capacities that condition what is or isn't perceptible is circumspect since such attempts limit what is and what is not a relevant appearance or sound — in the manner, say, that compression ratios for the transmission of conversations over a telephone line work in such a way as to minimize the amplitude of tone, voice, and other noises deemed unnecessary qualities of communicative experience so as to transmit a signal.[18]

What I have just described is the operation Rancière calls *dissensus*, which, as Frances Ferguson rightly notes, is "the basis for an abstract modeling of politics and has made politics susceptible to a schematic and spatial representation that involves minimal attention to specific political content or issues."[19] Dissensus is not a term that determines either the content of a concept or the normative elements of a practice. Rather it registers the fact of indistinction as a force that troubles political ambitions of commonality: aesthetic works have no ground for legitimating their stature as works of art, and collective forms of being are devoid of final appeals to right action in and for the collectivity.[20] The impropriety of the discrete, unauthorized gesture — the *ignorant gestu*, if you will — marks the condition of possibility for democratic participation and equality.

To consider Rancière's sentiments is thus to consider his manners of impropriety. As I suggest throughout, Rancière is a contrarian and his oeuvre gives emphasis to ways in which propriety is undermined as a mode of decorum or as a normative system for the assignment of persons in places and times. As I see it, Rancière's manner of impropriety is at the heart of his logic of emancipation to the extent that social and political emancipation for him occurs when the system of relations that determine concrete conditions of individual and collective existence are refigured. Hence the perpetual simultaneity of aesthetics and politics. As I noted in the preface to this book, the work of politics is first and foremost the work of dismantling the privilege of judgment as a model of social valuation and political participation. Judgments rely on criteria, and criteria are the currency of the entitled, that is, those whose pedagogical and social stature entitles them to make proclamations about the hierarchy of values. Thus the charm and attraction of a figure like Joseph Jacotot is not simply the charm and attraction of the eccentric populist.[21] Jacotot matters to Rancière in the same way that he mattered to the Communards of the Paris Commune: he matters because Jacotot develops an account of equality that refuses the propriety of judgment as a condition of political participation by refusing a priori common standards, including the common standard that to be an eligible participant in politics one must have a faculty of judgment.[22] And that refusal comes not with a declamation of social injustice but with participation in improper modes of doing and learning that show how there are no necessary ways of arranging things; that a pedagogical enlightenment can, itself, be improper; and that the coordination of a collectivity like a scholarly canon or a curriculum or any scenography of things can exist without having to adhere to accepted principles of organization. The form of propriety that privileges judgment as necessary to politics is simply that: a privilege of those who have already accepted the faculty of judgment as necessary to aesthetics and politics.[23] In contrast, the manner of impropriety that is at the heart of Rancière's sentiments affirms that there is no necessary order for the coordination of persons, places, and things — including an order of thinking that prioritizes reflexivity and judgment.

Consider in this context Rancière's emphasis on the "excess of words" in discussing the democratic revolutions of the eighteenth century in *The Names of History* or the importance he'll give to the force of "disjunctive conjunction" in Jean-Luc Godard's montage techniques.[24] In both these moments (discussed extensively in chapter 3) Rancière wants to register how the disfiguration of a particular way of arranging things is enabled by pushing on the limits of accountability inherent in an existing order. In the case of the democratic revolutions of the eighteenth century the political order of rule that attached the power of speech to the inheritance of nobility was disrupted by the explosion of voices that rearranged the relation of words and things and, in doing so, made apparent that "no primeval legislator put words in harmony with things."[25] Simply put, the order of authority that assigned a right of authorship (of words and deeds) was disfigured. Similarly, in the case of Godard's montage techniques, the relation between cut and continuity that was the basis of narrative cinema is disfigured, the cut itself is put on display through the repetition of a temporal jump, and the aesthetic ambitions of Aristotelian dramaturgy are turned upside down.

I should note at this point that Aristotle's *Poetics* is an important reference point for me in thinking about Rancière's aesthetics and politics, and it is a reference I carried with me throughout the writing of this book. This is another point of connection between Rancière's thought and the sentimental writers of the eighteenth century, who, for their part, did what they could to undermine an Aristotelian-Thomist notion of natural sociability.[26] The reason Aristotle's *Poetics* matters to Rancière is because in that work Aristotle establishes a formal system of representation that requires the delimitation of discrete activities called "action" and their installment in their proper place along a linear plot sequence. In short, the *Poetics* is the archetype of an arrangement of perceptions and sensibilities that labors to produce an account of proper fit. And it does so by relying on a specific sense of temporal continuity grounded in the notion of narratocratic teleology. Anything that doesn't fit within the system of arrangement of words and deeds that is Aristotelian dramaturgy simply does not count as representable.

Now it's not simply the case that Rancière is critical of Aristotelian poetics, though that is abundantly verifiable throughout his oeuvre, as I show in chapter 2. More exactly, Aristotle's hylomorphism, which aligns form and content, words and deeds, perceptions and sensibilities, is the ground of what Rancière will call the representative regime of the sensible, which, he claims, is also a normative regime of political access. The shift that Rancière's work traces from the representative regime of the sensible to the aesthetic regime of the sensible coincides with the emergence of modern democracies in the West, and it is a shift that registers political emancipation as an undermining of the Aristotelian emphasis on proper fit and right action. The part of those who have no-part, that is, the abstract political subject of Rancière's aesthetics and politics, stands as the occupational force of agency that registers improper capacities enacted by those persons and things who are not entitled to act.

This, in part, is why the category of the artisanal is ubiquitous throughout Rancière's writings. It is yet another site of his sentiment of impropriety. His writings are populated by aesthetic works made by individuals, from cobblers to parlor dancers, who blur the lines of official knowledge and skill. Or, better put, the artisanal (like the categories of the decorative, the ornamental, and the cinephile, also available throughout his oeuvre) is a category of uninitiated and autodidactic culture-making that Rancière places alongside official training in the arts (in the manner in which he places Jacotot's radical pedagogy alongside Althusser's scientism).

The artisanal is an important category not only for Rancière's own aesthetics and politics but for the historical and cultural trajectory that informs much of his thinking. As I noted, and as many others also have noted, Jacotot is an archetype for Rancière. But he was also an archetype for a nineteenth-century Parisian political imaginary that attempted to undermine the cultural imperialism of the time. As Kristin Ross shows, appeals to Jacotot were pervasive during the time of the Paris Commune, especially at its origin, when Gustave Courbet sent out a call to artists on April 6, 1871. The idea was to establish a system of total emancipation from the patronage of the Second Empire so as to liberate artists from social and political control. The initial call mentioned painters and sculptors as the artists in question (not surprisingly, given Courbet's predilections for the fine arts). But it was Eugène Pottier who took over the April 14 meeting and read out his manifesto that proclaimed a "rallying of all artistic intelligences."[27] This mattered because, as Adam Rifkin has shown, painting and sculpture had a privileged stature vis-à-vis censorship rights at the time.[28] Other arts, including the decorative and artisanal crafts, were easily susceptible to accusations of immorality in a way from which sculpture and painting were immune. Moreover sculptors and painters had a legal right to sign their names on their works; their propriety was their legal property.[29] But designers and drawers who participated in the production of statues by drawing up the prints for the foundries that would then produce the sculptures, for instance, didn't share that right and so could not claim economic benefit for their work. These artisanal workers did not, under

Rancière's terms, have a part in the system of artistic production. Their labor did not count; they were a part who had no-part in the recognized structures of artistic labor. The artisanal, in other words, is one of those aesthetic and political categories that, for Rancière, is an archetypal site of the inequality of practices and intelligences, of the affective pragmatics of impropriety. For what Pottier's manifesto ultimately declared was the impropriety of specialization.

Aesthetics for Rancière thus does not register a mode of inquiry that attempts to coordinate the social assignment of taste or the elaborations of qualifications and criteria for judging what is beautiful. Rather aesthetics names the affective pragmatics for the realignment of the dynamics of sensibility that render anything whatsoever or anyone whosoever sensible and thus perceptible. In short, the aesthetic regime of the sensible that Rancière traces as emergent parallel to the age of democratic revolutions of the long eighteenth century describes a force of equality for the appearance of words, deeds, sensibilities, and perceptibilities. This is why, in the end, aesthetics is always political and politics is always aesthetic: because any system of representation is a carrier of a normative set of assumptions about political inclusivity and exclusivity expressed in terms of who or what counts as worthy of perceptibility and sensibility. And given that the formal conditions of any system are such that it reaches its limit at the point when the propriety of its principles of organization fall short of establishing legitimacy of the system in perpetuity, then transformation is possible.

By determining the importance of aesthetics for politics, what Rancière traces is not the political importance of acts of judgments. A judgment is merely the representation of an experience that determines which objects are worthy of sense-making and intelligibility. His concerns lie elsewhere, in that inattentive moment that precedes judgment—a presubjective, but also preobjective, moment when the distensions of sensation have yet to assign value to specific persons, things, and events. This is the aesthetic moment of indistinction, which is also the political moment of equality, when anything whatsoever or anyone whosoever can count.[30] Indistinction undoes the Aristotelian aesthetico-political formula of decorum by making it so that anything and everything can make a perceptible difference because anything and everything can be a part since the extant conditions for partaking remain unassigned. Here the "measurelessness of the mélange" marks an interval in judgment's urge to direct perception and attention, thereby enabling a transformation of the possible.[31]

In important and compelling ways, then, Rancière's aesthetics and politics are a provocation to alter contemporary critical discourse in the face of that discourse's commitment to the subject/object distinction. His critique of Althusser's theoreticism is one instant in a larger series of concerns he expresses regarding the status of criticism (literary, political, etc.) as a tool deployed to impose rather than eliminate inequalities. At its most basic, Rancière sees contemporary critical discourse, especially those scientistic forms of cultural Marxist analysis that rely either on ideology critique or reification theory, as establishing epistemic qualifications for political emancipation, as if in order to be free, you must free yourself of your reveries and stop experiencing the world as you do so that you may know the world as it ought to be known. Freedom, in other words, can come only with knowing the world correctly. Rancière finds such critical moods in Althusser's theory of interpellation and the epistemic break hermeneutic for reading Marx, but he also considers these as available in a certain kind of critical stance that accepts the status of the epistemic as the basis for the formulation of political insights.[32] The sovereign stature of critical epistemology is, for Rancière, yet another dividing line that adjudicates legitimacy to certain forms of experience at the cost of others, producing scenarios wherein those who cannot render their experiences intelligibly simply don't count.

No doubt this provides a substantial challenge to our appreciation of Rancière's works, especially since scholarship in the social sciences and humanities is de facto oriented toward producing intelligibilities in the form of interpretations and understandings.[33] And it presents equally robust challenges to our appreciation of what critical thinking might be like, given how accustomed we are to enacting and teaching critical reflection in the Porphyrian mode of epistemic analysis. Throughout his oeuvre Rancière resists the privilege of the epistemic as both the root for and a branch of political thinking, and he does so by persistently offering up to readers scenes that can't be judged or interpreted but are nonetheless available to experience because they are affective in their transformation of sensibilities. He eschews the relentless predation of intelligibility via an equally relentless practice of description, aided by a prodigious deployment of *style indirect libre* (free indirect discourse).[34] This is what is at stake in his scenographic mode and his affective pragmatics, that is, to develop a critical milieu that positions things that typically don't belong together alongside (rather than against) one another, generating multiple moments of unweaving, through improper forms of solidarity. Such is the nature of Rancière's aesthetics and politics.

Consider in this regard one last example, Rancière's scenography of "divided beauty" and his treatment in *Aisthesis* of Johann Winckelmann's discussion of the Belvedere Torso. With *Aisthesis* we are dealing explicitly with scenography as both mood and mode of political writing: Rancière's book is written in fourteen discrete scenes, and each scene is explicitly *not* meant to be illustrative of an idea. The aesthetic here does not operate as representative of anything. Unlike Martha Nussbaum, for instance, who will claim a purposiveness of the literary in terms of the propositional character of stylistics (as when she says that "any style makes, itself, a statement"),[35] Rancière denies such purposiveness to his scenographies. For him a scene is "the optical machine that shows us thought busy weaving together perceptions, affects, names and ideas, constituting the sensible community that these links create, and the intellectual community that makes such weaving thinkable. The scene captures concepts at work, in their relation to the new objects they seek to appropriate, old objects that they try to reconsider, and the patterns they build or transform to this end."[36] So, how is the Belvedere Torso scene arranged and what does it render thinkable?

It is a scene that displays the inactivity of a part that has no-part (see figure I.1). The object of the scene, and the scene's arrangement, posits a break in the sensible regime of representation through the advenience of the aesthetic regime of the sensible: the break breaks with the privilege of sculpture within the hierarchies of the arts. What we have in view with the Belvedere Torso is not simply a mutilated statue but a statue afflicted by the injuries of time that have transformed it into a found object, a ready-made. There is no grandeur of Greek Antiquity here but the most ruined of found ruins. And Rancière places this ruin alongside the rediscovery of Ancient Greek Art as if to ask, How much ruin is necessary before we must accept that there is no longer a work of art here?

The scene itself works as allegory for the finitude of the logic of representation in democratic systems of government. In order for democracy to happen, according to Rancière, the form, function, and status of repre-

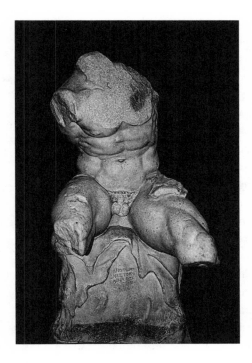

FIG. I.1 — The Belvedere Torso.
Photo by Jean-Pol Grandmont /
Wikimedia Commons.

sentation as the modes in and through which persons, events, and things
are made sensible are overturned. This posits the at once paradoxical and
counterintuitive idea that the rise of democracy announces the limits of
representation itself. That is to say, democracy emerges when the hylomorphic relation of form and content in representation is no longer viable
because the force of efficient causality that sustained the function of representation is dissolved. This centrifuge of relationality is a characteristic of
the aesthetic regime of the sensible, which, it's worth repeating, coincides
with those incipient democratic moments that disarticulate extant structures of and commitments to representation as the ground of political authority.

The scene of "divided beauty" regards a broken statue of an illustrious
figure, known for his heroic labors, whose ability to act has been mutilated,
as has our possibility of viewing him as the archetype of heroic agency. The
Belvedere Torso is the statue of a Hercules with no head, arms, or legs, sitting, and not doing anything. It overturns the ambitions of Aristotelian
dramaturgy because here we have an inactive, inert agent who is doing

nothing. Treatments of the statue up until Winckelmann's commentary (in his second volume of *The History of Art*, 1764) tried to persuade audiences that there was a purpose to the work, that the Belvedere Torso intended to show action of some kind, even of the contemplative variety. Some artist had even tried to complete the figure by imagining it as a sitting statue of a hero who had accomplished an action. Not only a hero, then, but a successful one too. In other words, some artistic and critical renderings attempted to recast the work as purposeful. But Winckelmann, Rancière tells us, refused to compensate for the lack that is the mutilated no-part, insisting, "There is no action to imagine."[37] Indeed the statue is pure inactivity because "a mutilated statue is not only a statue lacking parts. It is a representation of a body that cannot be appreciated any longer according to two main criteria used by the representative order: firstly, the harmony of proportions — that is to say, the congruence between parts and the whole; secondly, the expressivity — that is, the relation between visible form and a character — an identity, a feeling, a thought — that this visible form makes recognizable in unequivocal traits. It will be forever impossible to judge."[38]

The subject of this scene could just as easily be a political system. Indeed for Rancière it is, because the subject of the scene is not the statue itself but the collapse of an entire way of ordering the world, or, better put, the scene that has the mutilated statue as one of its parts portrays the dissensus of sensorial and perceptual organization. But more than that, the mutilated statue in Winckelmann's work is the site for the impossibility of judgment in the face of something that has no purpose, meaning, or interest. The Belvedere Torso doesn't simply lack parts; it lacks the necessary conditions for parts to relate to one another so as to count as either purposeful or meaningful — neither coherence nor contiguity, nor consensus nor proportion, nor purpose nor necessity, nor any other principle of cohesion suffices to warrant a judgment. The Belvedere Torso is, for Rancière, "radically insufficient," and this radical insufficiency "corresponds to the structural breakdown of a paradigm of artistic perfection."[39] In the face of the mutilated statue, the extant criteria for judging beauty — the harmony of forms and their expressive powers (i.e., the Aristotelian ideal of representation defined in terms of the correct relation of form and content) — are broken, disassembled, and made ineffectual. In one word: disinterested.[40]

And yet the object works. Somehow. It possesses an active element (or more than one?) imminent to the possibility of the scene. To paraphrase

Jane Bennett's political ecology of things, the scene of the Belvedere Torso makes available the statue's vitality intrinsic to its materiality.[41] It's not just the case that the part that has no-part is decidedly not inert because of (or as a function of) its brokenness. On the contrary, the no-partness is the condition of possibility for activity itself, an activity or vitality that has no purpose. With this in mind, one could go so far as to provoke this consideration: the conspicuousness of the Belvedere Torso is such that what is disclosed in the scene is the vitality of a nonsovereign collective agency beyond the ideal of a coordination of wills.[42]

Thus when I say that the mutilated statue is a part that has no-part, I mean to highlight the extent to which the aesthetic and the political are superimposed upon one another in Rancière's thought in very explicit ways, to the point of being genuinely indistinguishable. That's all very well and good. But we have yet to consider the effects of the scene and answer the question What does the scene do? The short answer is quite simple: the scene — and the scenographic per se — does nothing other than arrange and dispose elements. Rancière's writing, in other words, is not oriented toward the making of a justifiable argument whose purpose it is to give reasons to think or act in a particular way. It is instead a writing that puts on display an arrangement of perception and sensation. In this respect the connection that David Owen and Jonathan Havercroft make between Rancière's scenes and Wittgenstein's notion of aspect-dawning is entirely apropos. The force of that affinity lies in the fact that neither Rancière nor Wittgenstein requires "a substantive principle that can be stated independently and in advance of the particular disputes within which it is manifest."[43] I would extend this further, as I have elsewhere, and say that the sensible world of the manifest is the site for an aesthetics and politics.[44] That is to say, the scene renders remarkable an aspect in a manner akin to how Wittgenstein makes the remarkability of things an event, as when he says "Don't take it as a matter of course, but as a remarkable fact, that pictures and fictitious narratives give us pleasure, occupy our minds."[45] For both Rancière and Wittgenstein, what is remarkable (i.e., in both the sense of something being appreciable and what gives us pause to regard) is the vitality of the manifest.

The Belvedere Torso scene manifests a part that has no-part that interrupts an established way of organizing the proper relation between form and function, action and purpose. The representative regime of the sensible that expects action to be heroic, expressive, and meaningful is torn apart by the advenience of a ready-made, found object that cannot express anything and does nothing but changes everything. (As we shall see in chapter 4, "doing nothing" is an important mode of aesthetic and political action for Rancière.) The scene of the Belvedere Torso displays an artifact becoming media. And Rancière projects this becoming media through discrete acts of assembly that collect individual parts in order to compose themselves as a scene: the statue, the piece of writing, the cultural milieu, the criteria of judgment, and the structures of experience that legitimate interest (i.e., interest in the object, interest in the beautiful, interest in value, etc.). The scene calls for a division of all those elements that, up until that point, had authored the propriety of judgment. It is, in short, a scene of impropriety that recalibrates the relations of discrete units that constitute a collectivity grounded in "division, not completion";[46] to wit, the Belvedere Torso scene manifests a parsing of the sensible.

To the extent that politics is an activity of organization it is aesthetic because scenographic. And this is the way Rancière's writings are simultaneously political and aesthetic. They show the transformations of the sensible through acts of articulations of solidarity that admit of perceptibilities and sensibilities that undo authoritative structures of belonging. Equality is the operation of undoing, or dissolving, the structures of necessity that authorize the emplotment of persons, places, and times; this is the operation of dissensus. It is this manner of impropriety that I peruse throughout *Rancière's Sentiments*.

In this book I try to show the interaction of all these dynamics so as to keep in play the simultaneity of Rancière's aesthetics and politics. Most of the time I do this at the cost of justifying his arguments, defending his political conclusions, defining the meaning of his terms, or attesting to their applicability through either endorsement or example. My mode of reading focuses on distending dispositions rather than stacking propositions; I privilege description over prescription. This is the sense of "sentiment" I work with throughout the book that informs both my mode of reading Rancière's works as well as my appreciation of the scenographic work of *dispositio* in his aesthetics and politics. The sentimental mode of reading I adopt thus seeks to articulate repeated combinations of the following insights about Rancière, implicit in my discussions above:

1. Everything and anything has the power of sensorial appearance.
2. The disposition or style or arrangement of things is of primary political importance.
3. Given 2, politics is aesthetic.
4. The site of political and aesthetic attention is the dividing line that relates persons, things, and events.
5. Meaning, explanation, intelligibility, and understanding are not the exclusive determinants of critical thinking in the social sciences and humanities.
6. Given 5, nonpurposiveness (or disinterest) is a real dimension of experience.

The first chapter, "Rancière's Partager," focuses on the variability of Rancière's notion of partager that I take to be central to his aesthetics and politics. I begin by unpacking some conventional senses of the term *partager*, which in French signifies both sharing and dividing. It is a liminal term Rancière employs throughout his oeuvre, and though it's convenient and accurate to call it a term, it is better to regard it as a sensibility that works to coordinate a whole series of critical practices and literary dispositions. So in the second part of chapter 1, I show how partager resonates throughout Rancière's writings as mood. In doing so I propose to consider Rancière's partager as the basis of his theory of radical mediation.[47]

In chapter 2, "Rancière's Police Poetics," I delve into Rancière's style of thwarting relations. Here I am most explicit about the centrality of Aristotelian poetics as one of the principal sites of repeated engagement throughout Rancière's oeuvre. Relying extensively on the work of Paul Ricoeur, I reconstruct the kind of reading of Aristotle to which Rancière is responding. There is a bigger story to tell here, which I don't recount for reasons of space and fit, that regards the postwar French political and aesthetic reception of and response to Aristotelian hylomorphism in philosophy, literature, and cinema. But the basic moral of the story is this: Aristotelian poetics is the prototype of bourgeois decorum that exalts the privilege of being over becoming. More to the point, in chapter 2 I elaborate what I take to be Rancière's most scandalous proposition: that political emancipation might have little to do with intellectual enlightenment.

In chapter 3, "Rancière's Style," I offer an extended discussion of the politics and aesthetics of Rancière's deployment of *style indirect libre*, or free indirect style. In this regard I focus on the role of Flaubert in Ranciére's thinking and posit Flaubert as an alternative Jacotot. Also in this chapter I expand on Ranciére's critique of intelligibility and understanding as fundamental to critical thinking. All of these combined elements labor to propose a way of doing critical work and reading theoretical writings as oriented to forms of relationality and assembly formation rather than treating works and concepts as objects of interpretation and application. I do this in order to give weight to Ranciére's own aesthetic and political ambitions of eschewing the purposeful in both thought and experience. This chapter elaborates what an unpurposive mode of critical inquiry might be like.

In the fourth and final chapter, "Ranciére's Democratic Realism," I focus on the place of reverie in Ranciére's oeuvre and how reverie is at the heart of his democratic realism. This is to say that I emphasize the work of dreaming in Ranciére's affective pragmatics, and I do so by elaborating his critique of the Marxist tradition, especially that line of Marxist critical modernism that, he claims, has dismissed reverie as a real political practice. Throughout I focus on some scenes in *Aisthesis* and on the project of that book more generally. The emphasis of the chapter is on the role that leisure plays in Ranciére's work as a way of undermining an extant partition of the sensible in modern life between those who are and those who are not entitled to take time.

Finally, a note on my writing: I try to write in such a way as to occupy the sentimental mood I find characteristic of Ranciére's oeuvre. This means writing with an awareness of the work of distension and extension as well as fluidity and interconnectivity. At times this leads to repetition, not so much of insights as to formulations and points of emphases. In the conclusion of the book I attempt to collect those flows as well as possible in order to consider what an aesthetics of politics not rooted in the representation of experience through interpretation and judgment might look like.

CHAPTER ONE

Rancière's Partager

IN THIS CHAPTER two scenes resonate throughout. One is from Rousseau's *Discourse on the Origins of Inequality*, and the other is Rancière's own declamation about his research ambitions throughout his career. In the very first sentence of part 2 of the *Second Discourse*, Rousseau deploys ekphrasis to describe a cartographic act and its aesthetico-political force, saying this: "The first man who, having enclosed a piece of ground, to whom it occurred to say *this is mine*, and found people sufficiently simple to believe him, was the true founder of civil society."[1] And now Rancière: "And this redistribution itself presupposes a cutting up of what was visible and what was not, of what can be heard and what cannot, of what is noise and what is speech. This dividing line has been the object of my constant study."[2]

I can't possibly claim that Rancière had Rousseau in mind when he wrote his statement of purpose in the afterword to the English edition of *The Philosopher and His Poor*, but it's also impossible for me to read these two formulations as if they were innocent of one another. For in both instances, and dramatically so, there is an alignment of forces and gestures, of activities and utterances, of vistas and sounds that coordinate a political cosmology of inequality as an aesthetico-political practice of line-drawing. Rousseau's man draws a line in the ground and, in doing so, grounds the relation of property to propriety through the orchestrated ensemble of a pictorial gesture, a technical design, and a performative utterance. Indeed it would seem that for Rousseau the cartographic is synesthetic in that it conjoins the pictorial and the aural, the seen and the heard. That technical design of enclosure delimits a propriety that is now bound to property. The cartographic and declamatory gestures are auto-authorizing acts that affirm and assert the existence of a sovereign author as well as the propriety of property relations (i.e., the *auctor* as property designer). The author isn't simply the one who says "This is mine"; he is also the one who inscribes territory by authoring his own self as a natural object. The gesture is thoroughly Adamic, and, as Rousseau remarks, it is also pedagogical: in order for the gesture to work, it requires a space of ignorance, of "simple" others.

Rancière's own phrase picks up on the aesthetico-political nature of Rousseau's Adamic line and its pedagogic implications. Here the act of naming and designating (i.e., the relation of self to territory, propriety, and property) is a lesson in orthodoxy that can only be undone by an act of radical mediation that disfigures the mode of pictorial seeing implicated in Rousseau's cartographic scene. The grounding line of property that authors the propriety of authorial subjectivity is a *partage* that mediates (i.e., both connects and divides and thus transforms) the nature of the elements arranged therein.

I propose that in Rancière's treatment of the *partager* of aesthetico-political sensibilities one finds his theory of radical mediation.[3] I consider the distensions of partager as central to Rancière's aesthetics and politics and to his affective pragmatics more generally.[4] Partager on my reading is less a conceptual concrescence than the predicate of unspecified labors of mediation where demarcated lines are reworked and repurposed — remediated, if you will[5] — to reconfigure spaces and times. Here mediation is not a term that marks the reproduction of an extant political order, nor does it denote a function for the transmission of values. Mediation for Rancière regards the work of transformation of an order's design in a way akin to how Rousseau's cartographic scene marks an ekphrastic moment of transformation of the relations among man, mine, ground, founder, sovereignty, property, and inequality.

I borrow the term *radical mediation* from Richard Grusin.[6] It is a term that Rancière doesn't himself use, nor does Grusin discuss Rancière's work in his treatment of radical mediation. That said, it is a helpful term to incorporate in my treatment of Rancière's aesthetics and politics because it provides access to the transformational properties of political participation and agency that are at work in Rancière's affective pragmatics. As Grusin accounts for it, radical mediation considers how the force of mediation in everyday life is not reducible to preestablished accounts of structure or change. "Mediation," he affirms, "should be understood not as a standing between pre-formed subjects, objects or entities but as the process, or action, or event that generates or provides the conditions for the emergence of subjects and objects, for the individuation of entities within the world."[7] Mediation is not that which mediates between hylomorphic forms, but is the operation of interstitial immediacy out of which forms individuate.

For Rancière partager is the aesthetic operation that rearranges the dividing lines that structure sociopolitical divisions; it is a spatiotemporal predicate of in-betweenness wherein he locates the subject of politics. "A subject," he writes, "is an *in-between*," and "political subjectivization is the enactment of equality—or the handling of a wrong—by people who are together to the extent that they are between."[8] We might be persuaded, then, to consider partager to be Rancière's effort to amplify Marx's concept of division (as in "division of labor") beyond the scope of political economics and class distinctions. That is, rather than marking definitive distinctions, a partager marks "a process of subjectivization" as "a process of disidentification or declassification" or a dissensus.[9] Rancière's own insistence is thus to show how every division is also a "partage du sensible"—at once a dividing and a sharing of the in-between. Partager is the dissensus in between division and sharing.

In this account of Rancière's theory of radical mediation, aesthetics matters to politics because the aesthetic marks the site for practices of reconfigurations of the sensible—what in the introduction I described as Rancière's artisanal sensibility. In contrast to theories of the aestheticization of politics that treat aesthetics as synonymous with ideology,[10] and thus as a source for the anesthetization of political agency through the stultification of intellectual autonomy, Rancière's sense of aesthetics refers to affective practices of sensorial reconfiguration that enable a radical mediation of the in-between of those dividing lines that authorize inequality. In the aspectual relation I set up earlier, Rancière is returning us to the "ekphrastic temptation" in Rousseau's account of inequality (i.e., the temptation of treating pictorial lines as if they were natural) and extracting from it the gesture of artisanal artifice that repeats itself at every juncture where distinctions and differentiations are drawn, ordered, and designated.[11] Notably the ekphrastic temptation of treating drawn lines as if they were natural (a temptation we might also call "Westphalian") is not, for Rancière, a cognitive illusion or an epistemic mistake. It marks, rather, a perceptual milieu of networked sensibilities subject to the radical mediation of the partager of "several names, statuses, and identities; between humanity and inhumanity, citizenship and its denial; between the status of a man of tools and the status of a speaking and thinking being."[12]

This chapter is divided into three parts, and each part raises some of the concerns spelled out in my remarks. In part 1 I work through Rancière's critique of Althusser's orthodoxy and the implicit critique of Althusser's theory of mediation therein. I want to pick up on the shift between the idea of mediation as a force of repetition and reproduction, a force that can be interrupted only by an orthodox way of knowing (i.e., the epistemic break), to the idea of radical mediation as a process of transformation through undetermined labors for the reconfiguration of the sensible. This is to say that I read Rancière's critique of Althusser's orthodoxy as a critique of his theory of mediation that (for the former) is a carrier of an orthodox lesson plan for sociopolitical emancipation that reduces political work to a single form of intelligence, namely the science of theory. Rancière's break from Althusser is not an epistemological break but a break with epistemology, and thus a break with the privilege of Althusser's reductionist account of political work as intellectual labor. Part 2 offers the reader an excursus on the definitional subtleties of partager as both a force of sharing and division; in French, the verb means both sharing and dividing. Here I'll indicate how partager's liminal stature is the marker of in-betweenness.

Finally, part 3 undoes the approach to conceptual clarification of the previous sections. Here I am interested in putting on display the networked distensions of partager in Rancière's oeuvre. To do so I must therefore shift my stylistics of reading and writing from a Porphyrian to a sentimental arrangement of terms that shows the dispositional distributions of senses in Rancière's conceptual morphology.[13] The processual dimension of in-betweenness at the heart of Rancière's theory of radical mediation requires that the terms of relation not be treated as transcendental and immobile but as elements or parts of a kinematic arrangement. The point here is a classically sentimental one: pace Aristotle, it is not just the ideas and the senses that are not innate, but the relations that conjoin or disjoin subjects and objects—the forces that generate relations of solidarity or dissidence, for instance—are equally not innate. So whereas some of the classical sentimental authors may have pursued what Hume called a "human science" for the discovery of natural sociability (Hutcheson, Hume, and Rousseau chief among these thinkers), Rancière radicalizes their insights by showing that sociability itself is an object of artisanal manufacture. In part 3, then, I show what the mode of radical mediation Rancière proposes does to the pedagogy of conceptual morphology, where not only the terms but also the relations between terms are subject to dissensus.[14]

PART 1: Rancière's Radical Mediation

It is important to point out that Rancière does not explicitly elaborate a theory of mediation—or at least, he doesn't refer to his account of partager as a theory of mediation. Rather his work enacts radical forms of mediation that transform the existing divisions of any aesthetico-political arrangement. And by "acts of mediation" here I mean that his work is occupied with instances of partakings in unspecialized capacities that restructure the perceptual milieu of any coordination of persons, places, events, spaces, and sensibilities. I explained in the introduction how these dynamics play themselves out in Rancière's discussion of the Belvedere Torso from *Aisthesis*. There he offers up an instance of radical mediation in terms of the effects of time's erosion upon a piece of stone. Geological erosion is a kind of automatic partaking that has no purpose; it is a practice of doing without a determined subject. But that erosion, and the razed statue that emerges from erosion's labors, transforms the figure of the heroic man of deeds into a found object, or a ready-made, that compels us to come to terms with the qualification of sculpture as a superlative form of art. The Belvedere Torso is a part that has no parts (no head, no limbs, no fingers, no groin, etc.) but that nonetheless capacitates an alteration to the extant distribution of perceptions that determine the relation between art and doing, and thus the relations of authority, action, qualification, and legitimacy. No human transformed the work from statue to found ready-made. It happened as a result of the automatic caprices of erosion. The result is the eruption of a becoming-sensible that queers the dividing lines correlating sensation and perception. It's not just that the Belvedere Torso changes late eighteenth-century conceptions of art. It is the case that after the Belvedere Torso, representational art no longer has the stature it could previously claim.

For Rancière, then, mediation is not reducible to either transmission or reproduction. It is a force of transformation. And this difference is what is at stake in his critique of Althusser's lesson in orthodoxy.[15] Rancière's polemic against Althusser has been well rehearsed in several publications, most recently in Samuel Chambers's *The Lessons of Rancière*.[16] The explicit issue regards the relationship between emancipation and enlightenment, that is, the expectation that emancipation regards "a specific scene for the effectivity of thought."[17] Here "effectivity" reports a causal dynamic where the purpose of critical thinking is to enact change through a kind of cognitive-behavioral therapy. To break with ideology it is necessary to change people's minds so they will interpret the world differently. Thus Althusser's theory of revolutionary emancipation requires a form of conceptual realignment that harmonizes the relationship of words and things so as to generate accurate representations of the world and thus restore what had been distorted by capital's exploitation. This is the function of Althusser's "epistemic break" (a term borrowed from Gaston Bachelard's philosophy of science that also influenced Thomas Kuhn's notion of a paradigm shift) that designates "the mutation in the theoretical problematic contemporary with the foundation of a scientific discipline."[18] The epistemic break will thus expose the illusion of ideology through a cognitive remapping of the world.

Much of Rancière's response to this account of ideology critique, and to the theory of mediation implied therein, is outlined in *Althusser's Lesson* and, earlier, in the essay "On the Theory of Ideology: Althusser's Politics," first published in 1970 in Argentina and based on a course Rancière taught the previous year at the Université de Paris VIII–Vincennes. This earlier publication coincides with the publication of Althusser's own important essay "Ideology and Ideological State Apparatuses" (1970),[19] which likely suggests that Rancière was not relying explicitly on any published account of ideology by Althusser when penning his own polemic. That said, what is immediately relevant is the extent to which the epistemic break as a scientific theory for the correction of a distorted picture of the world — or, better, a distorted signaletics — is also a science of reading. And as a science of reading, Althusser's epistemic break regards the correct transmission of knowledge so as to interrupt the subordination of ideological reproduction. He declares ideology nefarious because it is a form of repetition that reproduces (and thus calcifies) relations of exploitation. In this regard mediation is the force of ideology that functions as a mode of transmission through repetition and reproduction. All mediation is ideological mediation that, on this view, functions like a signal repeater.[20] Social values that are carriers of inequality are reproduced through the repetition of signaletics that ensure the intergenerational transmission of domination and exploitation. Hence the famous scene of subjectification as interpellation that comes with ideological recognition. Relations of domination are reproduced simply through the behavioral habit (i.e., unreflective repetition) of responding to the signal prompt of hailing. The dynamic is thoroughly cybernetic (i.e., it relies on a negative feedback loop), as is the system of relations that enables it. The trick for Althusser is to revoke that behavioral automaticity (i.e., the stimulus-response dynamics) by breaking the signaletic cycle of ideological reproduction. But that break cannot come with an alteration or transformation of the extant relations that guarantee habitual repetition. This is because for Althusser the dividing lines and the political relations of domination they determine are natural objects in the world.

For Althusser the problem of mediation is one of false homologies, and his account of political work regards intellectual intervention in order to establish true homologies, as Fredric Jameson helps explain. Jameson describes mediation as "the relationship between levels or instances, and the possibility of adapting analyses and findings from one level to another."[21] In short, inquiry into mediation is inquiry into relations, their nature, and their application. From the Althusserian position, some relations are natural to a specific form, while others are not. Mediation is thus the operation where false unities of relation and form (i.e., class relations) are repeated. Such false homologies are reproduced because institutions that promote them are extended through time in a manner akin to the ways in which property or intergenerational wealth is inherited, thereby reproducing class differences between generations.[22] This means that mediation is a kind of embedded code (as are all homologies) reproduced by an institutionalized mode of repetition endemic to the system.

Further to this, the political and philosophical problem of Althusserian mediation (defined in terms of habitual repetition and thus ideological reproduction) is a problem of unreflective immediacy.[23] Mediation enables false representations through its immediate effects, and this is as much an aesthetic problem as it is a political one because aesthetics under this schema regards an experience of immediate (and therefore unreflective or uncritical) absorption at the moment when our sensory apparatus is impacted by an external object whose function it is to transmit preexisting experiential arrangements. The possibility of escaping the homological feedback loop of ideology is rendered null and void given the absence of the necessary space of distanciation for critical reflection. The best we can hope for in mediation is the repetition of "unreflective unities."[24] If the dominant (and most successful) mode of reproduction is the proliferation of undifferentiable homologies, then political work must necessarily require the intellectual effort of breaking the terms of an ideological homology. Hence the effectivity of the epistemic break, which is a science of interpretation that quite literally breaks homologies by instituting spaces of difference in between the forces of repetition. In short, the epistemic break isn't simply the name of Althusser's interpretive method; it is also the political capacity he invokes to foil the nefarious effects of mediation. If mediation is reproduction qua repetition, then the epistemic break is the heroic act of a kind of cognitive-behavioral therapy that will produce true homologies.

This means that Althusser's revolution must be scientific before it can be political. Althusserianism does offer "a specific scene for the effectivity of thought,"[25] as I've noted; but more than this, it reduces political work (and thus political participation) to just one type of activity, namely a cognitive-behavioral practice of psychic shock. This, and only this, is what counts as legitimate political work for Althusser. This is how Rancière will account for Althusser's lesson in orthodoxy: he will read that lesson as a lesson in bourgeois decorum that privileges a proper and harmonious comportment of mind (i.e., the production of true homologies) so as to produce a harmony of social representations. And this formula remains entirely Aristotelian (as I will explain in chapter 2); that is, it is a political solution that presupposes an account of the right disposition of things, of a harmonious correspondence between substance and form, subject and object, politics and knowledge that wants to make these right relations the basis of political mimesis. The possibility of political emancipation for Althusser lies in the capacity of the system to imitate the mind's true homologies and thus create good rather than bad repetitions.

In his polemic Rancière raises a basic fact about what some political scientists call the "coordination problem,"[26] that political motivation, solidarity, and participation are inordinately difficult (if not impossible) when your sense of epistemic privilege allows you to presume that political subjects lack capacities, and that barring the availability of such capacities, whatever it is that political actors might labor to do to ameliorate their own standing is improper. Rancière's Althusser is committed to a specific account of authentic political work, and that account begins with telling participants that their labors don't count because they lack the necessary intellectual skills (i.e., the capacity for critical judgment) for political agency. Such a theory of political action, Rancière tells us, "died on the barricades of May 68," when Althusserianism became the basis for professorial castigations of anti-intellectualism directed at student activists.[27]

Where does all this leave us? Quite simply, with two competing theories of mediation. The first, Althusser's, identifies mediation as a transcendental force for the reproduction and transmission of signs and their relations, a force that can be stopped only by breaking the compulsive habit of repetition through proper training in a scientific theory of reading and interpretation—to wit, a critical science of judgment. A socioeconomic class is a distorted system of signaletics (or a distorted mimetic structure) that establishes unharmonious forms of relationality. The trick is to scientifically evaluate such a system of signs, adjudicate the yield point of the apparatus, and exploit that yield point so as to break the force of automatic reproduction. Such a dynamic of social and political engineering is represented in the term *apparatus* itself, a term that describes an architecture for the imposition of representational forms through time.[28] But what Althusser's engineering metaphor insists upon is the fact that effective action demands expert knowledge: one must have specialized knowledge of system mechanics and its technologies of data analytics in order to locate the yield point of any technical structure. Thus for Althusser the business of political revolution is a matter for scientific experts who have the knowledge to make sensible judgments.

It is perhaps for this reason that Rancière quite explicitly abandons the sensibility of and the term *apparatus* in his work and turns to a sensibility and language of the *dispositif*—a move that parallels Foucault's own adoption of the term *dispositif* and that Alain Brossat has rightly noted marks the emergence of a novel conceptual and theoretical imaginary that, "to put it bluntly, represents a movement from 'science' to 'politics.'"[29] Brossat's analysis is correct, but I think this lexical shift represents something more than a move from science to politics (although that is definitely part of it). For *dispositif* is also a term that connects the idea of a technical instrument to a distensive associative dynamic that, as I said in the introduction, is rooted in the Roman rhetorical tradition of *dispositio*, defined as the disposition or arrangement of worlds.[30] The term *dispositif* imagines a technical instrument as a device for the production of relational arrangements and precisely not an apparatus for the reproduction of transcendental homologies. Rancière thus distances himself from Althusser's transcendental orthodoxy by introducing the sensibility of the *dispositif* as a scenographic *techne* that is always adjusting and altering, always playing with the unnaturalness of relations.

In English translations of Rancière's work it is difficult to appreciate this subtle but significant shift, in part because the French *dispositif* is so often translated as "apparatus" since there is no adequate contemporary English term that renders the difference. And in Rancière's own work the term *dispositif* appears occasionally, as when he affirms his interest in "studying material forms of dominant thought . . . and the rationality of thought at work, as it is embodied in *dispositifs*, institutions, and—not least—in the words (stolen from the enemy, interpreted, transformed, inverted) constantly exchanged in the struggle."[31] The sensibility of a *dispositif* comes out strongest in Rancière's engagement with technical media like montage in film, *style indirect libre* in the modern novel, photography, sculpture, dance, noise, and so forth. Indeed it is possible to read the entirety of *Aisthesis* as a paean to the *dispositif* as an associative milieu of sensibilities and dispositions that challenge modernist accounts of apparatus theory, as when he affirms in the *prelude* to *Aisthesis*, "The network built around it [i.e., a given artistic appearance] shows how a performance or an object is felt and thought not only as art, but also as a singular artistic proposition and a source of artistic emotion, as novelty and revolution in art—even as means for art to find a way out of itself. Thus it inscribes them into a moving constellation in which modes of perception and affect, and forms of interpretation defining a paradigm of art, take shape."[32] I read the idea of a network built around an artistic event that inscribes a moving constellation of perceptions, affects, interpretive forms, and artistic paradigms as *dispositif*. Thus it is that in his discussion of each specific technical milieu in *Aisthesis* Rancière refuses to treat the trajectory of possible effects of a *medium* in either a determined or a teleological manner, which is to say that his sensibility of the *dispositif* refuses an apparatus theory committed to mediatic influence as domination through mass deception.

From a theoretical standpoint, this shift in medial sensibilities marks a move away from an account of transcendental forms as necessary to the operations of political representation and toward an account of sentimental dispositions and arrangements as the sources for problematizing the political effectivity of transcendental forms of political representation. But beyond this the shift also represents an affective pragmatics that thinks mediation not simply as "an influence machine" for the transmission of values but as the conjunction of dispositional forces that relate things to one another within an interstitial milieu where the nature of relationality itself is undetermined.[33] Rancière's *dispositifs* bespeak a sentimental emphasis on the unnaturalness of any and all relations, thereby abandoning the classical (Aristotelian) model of mimesis as the basis for all political relations. In its stead he proposes a radical theory of mediation as an affective pragmatics for the becoming-sensible of relations. This radical theory of mediation is what Rancière calls *le partage du sensible*, or a partition or distribution of the sensible, that considers the part-taking of a subjectivity of in-betweenness (i.e., the part of those who have no-part) that has no determinate capacities or qualifications.

PART 2: The Senses of Partager

Earlier I elaborated Rancière's notion of partager as his theory of radical mediation. Mediation for Rancière is not equivalent to the reproduction of relations of domination through time; it is the name given to artisanal acts of aesthetico-political dissensus that occupy and transform the lines of division in a systemic homology. For Rancière simply breaking a habit of thought is an insufficient strategy for all of the reasons he rehearses in his critique of Althusser's lesson in orthodoxy (and that he subsequently elaborates in *The Ignorant Schoolmaster*). This is because the problem of emancipation from inequality involves something other than solving a conceptual puzzle by the application of a scientific hermeneutic. In short, for Rancière the problem of inequality and emancipation is not a problem of political judgment but a problem of solidarity, occupation, and participation.[34]

At this point I want to spend some time elaborating the senses of partager, what the term itself means, and how it operates as a political term
of art in Rancière's oeuvre. In doing so I will rely on elements of my previous discussion in the hope of emphasizing not only the political activity
of mediation but the political affectivity of Rancière's conceptual innova-
tions. In this section, then, I explore Rancière's notion of partager by first
addressing the multiple meanings of the French verb; I then outline how
Rancière's partager is a dimension of his poetics of knowledge; and finally
I elaborate the explicitly political dimensions of partager.

I've already noted that the specificity of any one concept in Rancière's
lexicon is difficult to grasp and impossible to localize; as Rancière himself admits, "I don't speak for members of a particular body or discipline.
I write to shatter the boundaries that separate specialists—of philosophy,
art, social sciences, etc."[35] This holds especially true for the notion of partager, a conceptual innovation that invokes the conditions of sharing that
establish the contours of a collectivity (i.e., partager as sharing) and the
disunities and distensions of that same order (i.e., partager as division).
That the French *partager* means both "sharing" and "dividing" is significant
to Rancière's account of political emancipation and solidarity, to the extent
that much of his aesthetico-political project is about discovering the centripetal and centrifugal forces for the incipience of collectivization, where
no common standard or consensus is available to ensure political coordination. This is the endeavor of solidarity-building under conditions of incommensurability. But more than this, the coincidence of sharing and division
in partager further suggests the unnaturalness of any divisive line since any
line is not naturally divisive nor naturally connective but both a sharing
and a division. To recall the Rousseauvian ekphrasis invoked earlier, there
is a point at which the line drawn in the ground that establishes the divisiveness of property must be shared by both the property owner and the
person willing to accept the cartographic gesture. The outside edge of the
line belongs to the one who does not own the property, just as the inside
edge of the line is the owner's property/propriety, though it is impossible
to know where the division between inside and outside is to be located.
Thus the reality is that both owner and nonowner belong to the property
line; they share what divides them.

Political equality for Rancière thus begins with a denaturalization of the
dividing line between the sensible and the insensible. Thus the inequality of

a partager that establishes a hierarchy between those who know and those who do not know, between those whose speech makes good sounds and those whose utterances are mere noise, holds the potential for its own dissolution. If the dividing line is the point of contact between commonality and divisiveness that structures the dynamics of a partager, then Rancière always holds open the possibility of a political partaking by elements excluded from a determined system of distributions. The exclusiveness of a partition that divides legitimate and illegitimate modes of being always holds open the possibility of a dissensual partaking by those deemed illegitimate to the dominant political community. And this dissensual partaking is an act of radical mediation that transfigures the centripetal tendencies of social isomorphism.[36]

In order for a collectivity like a social system or a political group to exist there needs to be a frame of equivalences in place that establishes the relations of commonality between things. Such a collectivity is at once a spatial and temporal composition that has a series of set dispositions that compose its structure and an order that guarantees their proper functioning. The ability to share in this community of parts (i.e., to be a part) is rooted in distinct conditions of perception that establish a correspondence between an object's impression and its intelligibility. We can thus speak of a collectivity as comprising the set of concrete correspondences among knowledge, awareness, sound, sight, and so on — correspondences that count as the aesthetico-political preconditions for participation in politics. A political community thus holds its shape because these preconditions make some parts commonly sensible and others commonly insensible. The simultaneity of the sensible as what addresses the correspondence between the reasonable and the perceptible — or, better put, the idea that the sensible implies a condition of knowledge — is what Rancière means when he affirms that a partager "is the system of self-evident facts of sense perception that simultaneously discloses the existence of something in common and the delimitations that define the respective parts and positions within it."[37] If, however, we were to limit our understanding of partager to an isomorphic arrangement that imposes form and function upon heterogeneous elements, then we would be reducing our understanding of it to something like an Althusserian ideological apparatus, which, as we have seen, is unavailable to Rancière for all the reasons I outlined in the previous section. Thus the aesthetico-political challenge of Rancière's notion of partager is to introduce the possibility that there is a distensive range of affective practices that discompose the inequalities produced by such isomorphic structures.

"Politics," Rancière thus affirms, "is an activity of reconfiguration of that which is given to the sensible."[38] That is, the task of an aesthetics of politics is to engage the practices of transfiguration of what is given to sense perception. Politics is always an aesthetic activity, then, not because there is a specific aesthetic to politics nor because there is a purposiveness to aesthetic objects that is political, but because within any specific social arrangement there are elements that circulate but that don't settle into any specific compositional whole. And though a mediatory function of partager tends toward centripetal convergence, these sensible intensities may disrupt that tendency at any time by introducing "lines of fracture and disincorporation into imaginary and collective bodies. . . . They form, in this way, uncertain communities that contribute to the formation of enunciative collectives that call into question the distribution of roles, territories, and languages. In short, they contribute to the formation of political subjects that challenge the given distribution of the sensible."[39] Thus the same force of circulation that coordinates words and images cannot prevent those words and images from falling into the wrong hands, so to speak. Rancière specifies that "the concept of wrong is thus not linked to any theatre of 'victimization.' It belongs to the original structure of all politics. Wrong is simply the mode of subjectification in which the assertion of equality takes its political shape."[40] These wrong people who speak out of turn or incorrectly are the agents of a dissensus whose modes of partaking are illegitimate according to the reigning order of a common sharing. Thus what the affective pragmatics of partager ultimately afford is the possibility of an illegitimate partaking that results in the dissensus of a previous sensible regime.

Herein one also finds the prickly dimension—Rancière calls it the "polemical universal"[41]—of politics: equality is insensible. It arises whenever a sensual intensity appears and when the conditions of perceptibility for that sensual intensity need to be created rather than derived. To revert to one of Rancière's own favorite examples, the tale told by Livy of the plebian secession on Aventine Hill as interpreted by Pierre-Simon Ballanche, the quarrel between the Roman patricians and the plebs is not one between competing interests, or even between differing conceptual accounts of recognition. The contest, rather, is one over the conditions of a *partage*; that is, it is a polemical contention over whether there exists a common scene where the plebians and patricians might actually entertain one another as an "uncertain community."[42] As Rancière states, "There is no place for discussion with the plebs for the simple reason that plebs do not speak. They do not speak because they are beings without a name, deprived of logos — meaning, of symbolic enrollment in the city. . . . Whoever is nameless cannot speak."[43] This is not a scene of responsiveness but a conspiracy (in James Martel's sense of the word) of radical mediation.[44]

In other words, the polemical universal of equality is not rooted in the pursuit of a consensual agreement over disputing interests but in the dissent over the perceptual preconditions that make the noise coming out of one's mouth an utterance rather than a guttural sound, speech rather than noise, language rather than babble. The scandal of the plebs, ultimately, is that they took part in a mode of action to which they were not entitled; that is, by talking they enacted an improper partaking acting as if they had a name, as if they had the right to speak, the right to make promises, to express themselves. By taking those acts as their own practices, they disrupted (i.e., *partagé*) the order of the city and, implicitly, the order of propriety that structures the city's partager, thereby mediating the scene of contest and rearranging the conditions of perceptibility at that time and in that place.

"Politics," Rancière explains, "revolves around what is seen and what can be said about it, around who has the ability to see and the talent to speak, around the properties of spaces and the possibilities of time."[45] He concludes that through this partager in acts of appearing we have "the ground of political action: certain subjects that do not count create a common polemical scene where they put into contention the objective status of what is 'given' and impose an examination and discussion of things that were not 'visible,' that were not accounted for."[46] Rancière's partager might be reasonably configured as a rendering apparent of things previously insensible. But as we have seen, partager is only partly a political practice because it is also an aesthetic practice — and the combination of the aesthetic and the political creates a distensive coordination of activities that further illustrates the work of radical mediation that is at the heart of Rancière's aesthetics and politics. My point, therefore, is this: given this distensive dynamic, we can't simply rely on the Porphyrian model of conceptual diagnostics adopted in this section to unpack the content of Rancière's oeuvre. This does not get us far enough in appreciating the kind of aesthetico-political work partager affords; there is more conspiring to be done.

PART 3: The Resonances of Partager

In the previous sections I elaborated the conceptual connections among dissensus, partager, *dispositif*, and radical mediation in such a way that the complicity of these terms renders them almost interchangeable. Partager is the activity of dissensus that is the name Rancière gives to the affective pragmatics of radical mediation enacted via the scenographic dynamics of *dispositifs* that include (but are not limited to) the participation of that incipient political subjectivity he refers to as the part of those who have no-part (recall, once again, the Belvedere Torso example). Rancière's aesthetics of politics consistently reconfigures our inherited commitments to the naturalness of lines of division, chief among these being the partitions that consign political emancipation as tethered to a specific form of intellectual enlightenment.

Given this, it is admittedly difficult to articulate Rancière's critical project, considering contemporary accounts of the nature of critique as an epistemological enterprise.[47] He is decidedly not a critical theorist, with his rejection of the architectonics of critical theory, its epistemic privilege, and its aesthetic sensibilities. He is not interested in deriving or determining an ideal theory of politics, and he doesn't offer a constructive theory of meaning, nor does he offer a hermeneutic method. He is interested in solidarity, emancipation, and political participation. But he offers no game plan for how these might best be articulated or how they might come about. What he does offer is a formal engagement with works and their operations: texts, historical examples, physical objects, events, persons. And in all these engagements he distends a complex lattice of insights and observations that extend his sensibilities vis-à-vis a diverse archive of emancipatory capacities that is in a state of constant revision. In short, Rancière's critical activity is not normative but pragmatic, and it works by laying out through paratactic description and *style indirect libre* a series of disjunctive relations for things that have no reason for belonging together. His critical practice, in other words, is located in his own stylistic of presentation, his ways of reading works and of writing about them. Hence the insufficiency of the Porphyrian model of conceptual analysis for engaging his oeuvre. At the risk of repeating myself, it is important to keep in mind that Rancière does not offer a tree of political knowledge but a network of sensibilities.

Scholars typically read for understanding in a mode that John Guillory calls "intensive" and that "aims at analysis or interpretation."[48] And yet within Rancière's schema, where understanding counts less as an achievement than as an isomorphic qualification, reading for understanding is problematic. And it is clear—not so much from his mode of argumentation as in his style of writing—that he dissuades his readers from approaching texts exclusively as objects of understanding. One need only appreciate his deployment of *style indirect libre* to acknowledge the extent to which his own style of writing is dissuasive of understanding as a readerly ambition (more on this in chapter 3). This is why I say that a Porphyrian model of scholarly reading, where reading is oriented to a hierarchical organization of knowledge that wants to treat a work of writing as if it were a phylogenetic apparatus, is to be resisted when reading Rancière's oeuvre.

Manuel Lima has shown that the Porphyrian mode of representing understanding "is so ingrained in our minds that we employ it figuratively in a variety of daily circumstances, which in turn conditions the way we understand things and express them to others."[49] Consider how often we use such metaphors as "the root of the matter," "branches of government," "grassroots politics," or "stems from." More than ideational shortcuts these expressions point to a well-established, ancient system for classifying knowledge and understanding based on Porphyry's (234–ca. 305 CE) brief introduction to Aristotle's *Categories* (translated into Latin by Anicius Manlius Severinus Boethius, 480–524 CE). In those pages "Porphyry reframes Aristotle's original predictables into a decisive list of five classes: genus (*genos*), species (*eidos*), difference (*diaphora*), property (*idion*), and accident (*sumbebekos*). Most importantly, he introduces a hierarchical, finite structure of classification, in what became known as the tree of Porphyry, or simply the Porphyrian tree."[50] The Porphyrian tree represents knowledge as a formal system of interrelated parts that can be mapped and charted according to a hierarchical architectonic that takes as given both the nature of the parts and the relations between them. The Porphyrian tree thus gives us a data visualization for the emplotment of good thought (see figure 1.1).

In light of the difficulty of reading Rancière with the standard Porphyrian model of data visualization, I propose a different mode of scholarly reading indebted to Rancière's own theory of radical mediation. This mode of reading, which I have called the sentimental mode, does not take the structure and relation between terms and objects as given, nor does it presume understanding as reading's telos. Like the sentimentalist approach in general, such a mode of reading suspends the normative expectations of relevance for the selection of terms and concepts. In doing so it also suspends the naturalism implicit in the lines that connect terms, and thus the naturalism of Porphyrian relations. If the point of the Porphyrian model of knowledge visualization is to transmit a formal structure for the representation of proper understanding, the sentimental mode of reading invited by Rancière's partager is a distensive complex of interrelational adjacencies that procure a regard for the occurrence of an unforeseen.[51]

A visualization for sentimental reading might begin with the following exercise. Imagine you are reading a book and, as you read, you jot down in a notebook a single term or idea as it strikes you. Now imagine cracking the spine of that notebook so as to loosen and separate its pages and thus dissolve the sequence of the list.[52] This is a first step distancing us from the Porphyrian apparatus and its vertical lines so as to dissonate us from "the role taken on by the paradigm of the page in all its different forms, which exceed the materiality of a written sheet of paper."[53] Such a scholarly exercise "disturbs the clear-cut rules of representative logic that establish a relationship of correspondence at a distance between the sayable and the visible."[54] And that is

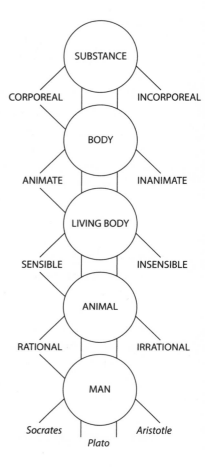

FIG. 1.1 — A Porphyrian tree as sketched by the thirteenth-century logician Peter of Spain. Line art redrawn by Christine Riggio.

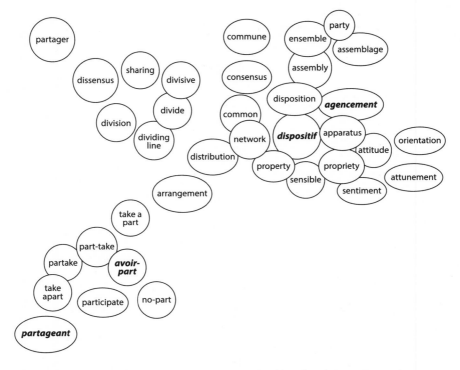

FIG. 1.2 — The senses of partager. Line art created and redrawn by Christine Riggio.

what a sentimental readerly mode tries to do: to break the isomorphic correspondences that take understanding as a telos. It's not that such a mode of reading refuses understanding as a scholarly ambition so much as it refuses understanding as an aesthetic paradigm for politics.

Let us proceed with our deforestation exercise. Now that we've disassembled the pages of the notebook, let's lay them on a scrim large enough to hold all of them; next, we'll shake the scrim, shuffling the pages and re-collecting them without paying attention to the order in which they've landed. The list on p. 38, "An Ecology of Resonances," and figure 1.2 contain an assemblage of words and adjacencies someone might jot down while working through some of Rancière's texts. Notice that these terms might or might not appear in the actual work, but they could nonetheless advene while one is reading the works.

partager	orientation	property
partageant	*avoir-part*	network
partake	division	sensible
part-take	take apart	arrange
dispose	take a part	participate
party	distribute	sharing
apparatus	assemble	dividing
distribution	*dispositif*	propriety
agencement	share	sense
assembly	dividing line	dissensus
commune	ensemble	insensate
communard	disposition	dispossess
sentiment	distension	
attunement	no-part	

Notice also that the order of the words isn't determined by any specific system of classification. These terms are resonantly adjacent and not logically or culturally adjacent, to invoke Michael Freeden's morphological analysis of ideational forms.[55] We might, in light of this exercise, consider adding a third condition of relationality to Freeden's own classification of political ideas: a resonant adjacency (i.e., *agencement*, Fr.) that emerges from a sentimental readerly mode, where no reason suffices to legitimate the connections, relations, proximities, and orderings — the conspiratorial arrangement[56] — of terms, objects, and perceptibilities. For that is the specificity of the *dispositif*: it is a milieu whose arrangement of parts is undetermined but is nevertheless effective in transforming the nature of classification and thus the relations of power that organize divisive distributions. Reading Rancière's oeuvre in this way—with a view to a dissensus of dispositional arrangements—involves having to draw lines of connection and division that are in no way natural to the terms themselves. The best you can do is coordinate a distension of denaturalized resonances that appear here and there throughout a work and that weave ideas, ambitions, perceptions, and sensations. Hence partager, which is neither a concept nor a category but an affluent node for an interconnected ecology of sensibilities and practices that at once assemble and dissonate vistas, auralities, perceptibilities, and relational forms.

In part 1 I offered insights into how Rancière's notion of partager may be read as his elaboration of a theory of radical mediation that alters the function of mediation itself from the reproduction of social relations to their transformation. This, I suggested, goes along with his scenographic ambitions throughout his oeuvre and his aesthetics and politics. In part 2 I related partager to dissensus by emphasizing its meaning as both a sharing and a division. Partager is the dissensus of a line that enables the divisive sharing of things, where sharing is possible because there are divisions. In part 3 I have tried to move beyond the readerly schematics of the previous two sections by showing how the Porphyrian mode of organization and understanding does not take into account the function of radical mediation that attempts to undo the isomorphic system of knowledge implicit in any mode of reading for understanding. To be sure, Rancière doesn't refuse understanding per se; through his own writing and stylistics, however, he refutes those "hierarchies of representation" that treat understanding as the telos of good thought.[57] In enacting such refusals through his own practices of writing and reading he claims to "establish a community of readers as a community without legitimacy, a community formed only by the random circulation of the written word."[58]

CHAPTER TWO

Rancière's Police Poetics

IN CHAPTER 1 I explored Rancière's account of social and political change as an account of the transformative powers of aesthetic mediation (i.e., the affective pragmatics of *partager*). In this chapter I will address the site of aesthetico-political occupation, namely Rancière's police poetics. The initial impetus for the elaboration of a poetics of the police was and is Althusser's lesson in orthodoxy, an orthodoxy committed to the idea that political emancipation necessitates a specific kind of intellectual and hermeneutic capacity (i.e., the epistemic break). But this lesson is not limited to the Althusserian project. As Rancière shows in many of his works, a police poetics is a general operation that regards a specific kind of power dynamic that codifies relationships between names and things. He will go on to name this dynamic "the mimetic order," or "the representational regime of the sensible," and he will invoke historical and contemporary examples that demonstrate the misguidedness of assuming that political capacities necessitate intellectual skills. The modern period is, for Rancière, an epoch of excess in skills, agencies, capacities, and partakings of dissensus that emerge as a result of the unweaving of mimesis. And as I've suggested, the ambition of Rancière's interventions is to show the possibility of a politics without mimesis.

Earlier I also suggested that Rancière's critical approach is difficult to grasp to the extent that it doesn't rely on interpretive prowess, intellectual competence, or the endorsement of the faculty of judgment. The *dispositif* of dissensus dissuades from such a critical apparatus, although traces of these capacities pepper his work throughout. The intensity of his critical energy comes in giving value (and thus attention) to the diurnal capacities of ordinary individuals who conspire to alter dispositional arrangements, as we see in his classic study of nineteenth-century worker-poets who rearrange their circadian rhythms so as to write, discuss, and daydream (though in their case it might be more accurate to call it an activity of "awake-dreaming" since their daydreaming took place at night).[1] Rancière's critical sensibility is thus distensive and committed to the occupation of a supernumerary excess of any and all forms of doing. The part of those who have no-part is the interstitial subject of politics that, quite literally, does not count because it is excessive to the extant modes of collectivization. It exists in between the system of qualifications of representation that "distributes ways of doing and making as well as social occupations."[2] The critical purchase of Rancière's aesthetics of politics is thus to show that no relation is fixed and necessary, so anyone or anything can occupy a variety of forms (of action, of sensibility, of perceptibility) that offer alterations to the legitimacy of an order and its criteria of qualification.

Another way of stating this is that for Rancière a central aesthetic and political site of engagement is decorum. Decorum refers to the expectations of comportment, mores, and sensibilities in an isomorphic social structure. It is a term that indicates a system of behavior, the expectations of behavior, but also a principle of organization. The Latin root of the term *decorum* (*decere*, meaning "to adorn or grace") is found in the English *decorate*, which refers to diurnal practices of ornament but also to the honorific title given to the doers of great deeds.[3] We decorate military personnel so as to acknowledge and praise their heroic actions, for instance, and in doing so, we establish certain actions as more valuable than others, as in Horace's famous phrase "Dulce et decorum est pro patria mori" (Ode, III:2:13 — "It is sweet and becoming to die for one's country"), subsequently reimmortalized in Wilfred Owen's famous (and ironic) redeployment of the expression in his World War I poem "Dulce et decorum est." Decorum is also one of the governing virtues of classical rhetoric that Nancy Struever identifies as "the most crucial" of all the rhetorical canons for Renaissance humanists: "Since the Humanists' critical apparatus was rhetorical analysis, the concept of decorum became the framework of their attempts to establish internal coherence in their texts."[4] And as Robert Hariman also proposes, echoing Struever, decorum is a dominant political style that insists on an aesthetic sensibility which deems proportion and due measure virtues of speech and politics.[5]

For Rancière decorum is the sensibility of the police. It refers to specific regimes of sensorial arrangement and comportment (which he will ultimately identify with Aristotelian mimesis) committed to the right disposition of capacities and subjectivities in a social order.[6] It is synonymous with proper fit and with a concordance for ordering actions according to a system of correspondences of space, place, time, and way of doing. If, as we saw in chapter 1, Rancière's aesthetic and political agenda is dedicated to dis-sensing the dividing lines in any social order, then decorum is the force that grounds the efficient causality of those dividing lines. Here, then, is Rancière on the relation between mimesis and decorum:

> Aristotle rejects the conflation Plato plays between two kinds of imitation, that of the poet offering fables and characters and that of the soul acting or suffering according to the models that have been imprinted in it. Plato tied these two imitations together in a single theory of identification, according to which the theatrical simulacra of imitation were necessarily transformed into disturbances in the soul. Aristotle separates them and, rather than making the polity and the soul into true poems, circumscribes the place of *mimesis* among the activities of men and the occupations of the polity. He challenges the passive status of *mimesis* that led Plato to see it as a simulacrum leading to suffering, and instead gives it an active status as a mode of knowledge, which is inferior but still real. He can then define a system of legitimacy for *mimesis* on this basis: first, a positive virtue of the act of imitation as a specific mode of knowledge; second, a reality principle for fiction that circumscribes its specific space-time and its particular regime of speech (and the all-too-famous *catharsis* designates above all this autonomy of the effects of speech, this way of confining tragic emotion to the stage); third, a generic principle that distributes modes of imitation as a function of the dignity of their subjects; fourth, criteria for judging whether fables are suitable or unsuitable for tragic or epic imitation. He thus defines the first elements of the system of representative decorum that

will be systematized by the classical poets of representation. He also founds the principle of the presence of speech that will form the frame of the poetics of representation by creating a harmony between the reality principle of fiction, which circumscribes a specific space-time, its particular regime of speech, and the inclusion of this speech in the rhetorical universe that conceives of speech in the assembly or tribunal as social action.[7]

I can think of few passages in Rancière's oeuvre that capture as precise a sense of the operational logic of a poetics of the police as this account of Aristotelian mimesis and its relation to modern decorum. The objective of this chapter, then, is to unpack this sensibility and its operation throughout Rancière's oeuvre.

I offer a reconstruction of Rancière's Aristotle by elaborating Aristotle's theory of emplotment (or *muthos*). I then show that emplotment is the basis for a theory of decorum defined as a normative account of good fit. I do this by reading Aristotle's *Poetics* in tandem with his *Metaphysics* (especially book 7). What these two works offer is a way of conceiving of a kernel of action as an identifiable and specifiable essence that may be fit into a sequential line called a plot. A good representation, by which Aristotle means a representation worthy of imitation, is determined by the coordination of action, character, and sequence that articulates an account of emplotment as good fit. Good fit establishes a line of connection between proper action and good sense (i.e., "good sense" is the English translation of the French *le bon sens*, that is also the French term for the English *consensus*). This account of fit as the right disposition of actions *is* decorum, a relational dynamic that naturalizes the dividing lines of social qualification for what can be seen, said, and done and by whom.

Invoking a different vernacular elaborated by Jacob Levy, we can describe Rancière as concerned with the problem of aesthetic and political isomorphism that he locates in the tradition of Aristotelian decorum.[8] And like others with similar concerns, Rancière's aesthetic and political perspicuity attends to the intermediary spaces that dislocate isomorphism. In the second part of this chapter I focus on Rancière's *The Names of History* and *Film Fables* to show the various strategies for interrupting isomorphism. *The Names of History* problematizes the commitment to political representation in light of the democratic revolutions of the eighteenth century that, according to Rancière's study, broke with the representational regime of the sensible. From a more technical, though no less formal perspective, *Film Fables* engages the technicity of cinematic montage, especially Jean-Luc Godard's montage sequences, to further frustrate decorum's isomorphism. What the democratic revolutions of the long eighteenth century ultimately do in breaking with the representational regime of the sensible is make it so that the montage cut in the editing room dissolves efficient causality as the normative standard for thinking about relationality tout court. Like the Belvedere Torso, the montage cut is a part that has no-part whose status as an amorphous interstice capacitates the transfigural forces of radical mediation. If decorum thus stands as a poetic qualification of proportion and fit for political action prior to the eighteenth century, then part of Rancière's aesthetic and political project will be to occupy capacities that thwart the normative demands of decorum.

PART 1: Aristotle's Decorum

I propose a reading of Aristotle's metaphysics of substances (or hylomorphism) alongside his poetics of mimesis that will help substantiate Rancière's poetics of the police. The question I try to answer is this: What kind of Aristotle is Rancière working with, and how does that Aristotle come about? To be sure, I don't pretend that this is a universally accepted reading of Aristotelian mimesis.[9] I do suggest, however, that this is an Aristotle that is available in Rancière's work and that this Aristotle helps us better grasp the force of Rancière's own aesthetic and political commitments. I begin by outlining some important aspects of both the *Poetics* and the *Metaphysics*. Reading these two texts together is productive because whereas the *Poetics* gives us a theory for the coordination of action, character, and time, the *Metaphysics* offers an account of how we might conceive of action as an essence, or a discreet and bounded unity—a point—that may be plotted along a temporal axis. These two aspects of Aristotelian thought complement and build on each other to afford an account of mimesis as a normative theory of good action and good works, and an account of action as at once visible and measureable.

Aristotle begins the *Poetics* by affirming that the task of writing is to imitate and that "the objects the imitator represents are actions."[10] Imitation is "natural to man from childhood."[11] This means that what are imitated (i.e., actions) are the objects of writing. And so on Aristotle's own account what the *Poetics* offers is a theory of technical objects, their properties, their structure, and the formal principles for their arrangement. "In poetry," Aristotle will thus affirm, "the story, as an imitation of action, must represent one action, a complete whole, with its several incidents so closely connected that the transposal or withdrawal of any one of them will disjoin and dislocate the whole."[12]

The structure of the plot regards the relationships of parts to whole, and every single part must do its job in order for the whole to work. What constitutes the nature of a good part is whether it is necessary, and the writer must always endeavor to represent only necessary things, otherwise she risks creating something merely episodic, by which Aristotle means disjoined and dislocated: "I call a Plot episodic when there is neither probability nor necessity in the sequence of its episodes."[13] And again Aristotle will go on to state, "The right thing, however, is in the Characters just as in the incidents of the play to endeavor always after the necessary or the probable, so that whenever such-and-such a personage says or does such-and-such a thing, it shall be the necessary or probable outcome of his character; and whenever this incident follows on that, it shall be either the necessary or the probable consequence of it."[14] The task of the poet, then, is to arrange actions that obey the demands of necessity or probability. And this is the crucial point: the dark space in between events and that sequence of events must be governed by necessity or probability. The capacity to create such relations determines the poet's skill as a "maker of likenesses."[15] The alternative is fragmented episodes that are decidedly *not* the mark of a good work.

As we shall see, this robust sense of connectivity is what is at stake in Rancière's account of the rise of the commons and in his account of cinematic montage. That is, the matter for Rancière regards putting pressure on the conviction that connectivity between individual entities (shots, actions, persons) is assured and legitimated by the power of representation as the common sense for relating things that have no reason for belonging together. Aristotle's point is that anything disconnected or episodic lacks a purpose, and thus the possibility of sense, because sense is possible if and only if there is necessity or probability built into the spaces of intermediacy. Those actions that lack either purpose or necessity are insensible.[16]

The only time Aristotle interrupts this dynamic is in the case of metaphor, which is an unlikeness that nonetheless has the purpose of creating a new meaning. Aristotle famously defines metaphor tautologically: "Metaphor consists in giving the thing a name that belongs to something else; the transference being either from genus to species, or from species to genus, or from species to species, or on grounds of analogy."[17] The tautology, as Paul Ricoeur explains, regards the fact that the term *metaphor* is itself a metaphor of transposition (from the Greek *metapherein*, "transference" or "carrying over"). "To explain metaphor," writes Ricoeur, "Aristotle creates a metaphor, one borrowed from the realm of movement; *phora* as we know is a kind of change, namely change with respect to location."[18] Thus Aristotle invents a term to account for something that is fundamentally impossible to justify within his metaphysical schema: the transposition of essence from one substance to another. Metaphor accomplishes what nothing else can: it is a medium of transference that enables the movement of essence between substances. This is what the transposition of meaning that is the tropological function of metaphor stands for: an act of transubstantiation. It is no doubt for this reason that Aristotle will later assert that "the greatest thing by far is to be a master of metaphor. It is the one thing that cannot be learnt from others; and it is also a sign of genius, since a good metaphor implies an intuitive perception of the similarity in dissimilars."[19]

To recap, Aristotle's *Poetics* offers an account of parts (characters and actions) and whole (plot) and their combination, thereby providing both a theory of representation (mimesis) and a metaphysics of composition (emplotment as necessary or probable action). Character and action—the composite parts of plot—are elements in a sequential series that may be plotted along a line whose movement is at once causal and teleological because (if done well) all the collective elements count as necessary to the composite whole. This generates a sense of certainty for action, which is another way of saying that in the *Poetics* we are given an account of what good behavior is: the doing of a necessary action, at the right time, that makes sense. And all of this is representable in a work whose wholeness is a composite of necessary parts. This insight will prove fundamental to Rancière, who will acknowledge Aristotle's theory of mimesis as a theory of solidarity that determines the arrangement of persons and actions according to normative criteria of decorum.

Now the account that I'm providing of the *Poetics* works if we read it alongside the *Metaphysics*, especially book 7, where Aristotle elaborates his theory of Being defined as a composite of matter and form, or hylo-morphism. So to continue a reconstruction of Rancière's Aristotle, we must allow ourselves a readerly conceit and read book 7 superimposed on the *Poetics* and keep them simultaneously in mind. Such a readerly conceit enables us to see that Aristotle's invention of first principles is indebted and entangled with the theory of mimesis developed in the *Poetics*. First principles are "first" because the *Poetics* grants us an intuitive sense of first-ness as both a narratological and a temporal fact of due process, conti-nuity, or necessity. That is, we can accept the fact of first principles because the *Poetics* provides us with a temporal arrangement of order as beginning, middle, and end: "To be beautiful, a living creature, and every whole made up of parts, must not only present a certain order in its arrangement of parts, but also be of a certain definite magnitude."[20] Existence, as it is ac-counted for in the *Metaphysics*, is a whole made up of parts, and some parts precede others because existence for Aristotle "present[s] a certain order in its arrangements of parts."[21] The certain order or arrangement of existence thus requires of the philosopher the capacity to specify which parts pre-cede others in exactly the same way that the poet must determine the order of plot and the structure of emplotment. In short, existence is structured like a plot. In this regard we might consider the existence of substances equivalent to incidents in dramaturgy.

Several things are at play in this account of metaphysical emplotment and the movement of existence.[22] The first is that essence precedes exis-tence and that existence regards a sense of due process, or a "comes to be," as Aristotle refers to it in the *Metaphysics*: "Everything that comes to be comes to be by the agency of something and from something and comes to be something."[23] Simply put, being precedes becoming, and becoming has a plot-like structure: its movement is motivated by necessary or probable causes. This is what Aristotle calls "the process" or "active principle" of exis-tence.[24] And this active principle comes from substances; thus substances themselves are not and cannot be predicated on anything. We know that substances are primary things, "and primary things are those which do not imply the predication of one element in them of another element."[25] In this respect being is originary, and becoming follows from or is subsequent to it. We might say that becoming is the predicate of being and that there is such a thing as a true becoming: it is the constrained movement of purpose when an action predicates substance by necessity, as does a good plot. A false becoming, then, is unnecessary movement or insensible actions that are not part of the trajectory of purposive predication — to wit, the discontinuous or episodic.

Furthermore an action is a substance; it is the essence of energy: "That the movers are substances, then, and that one of these is the first and another a second according to the same order as the movements of the stars, is evident."[26] This is important to keep in mind as I continue to reconstruct an Aristotelian poetics in adjacency with the philosopher's metaphysics because the idea of movers as substances allows the possibility of conceptualizing action as a point in a plot sequence, or what Ricoeur identifies as Aristotle's theory of emplotment. This matters to Rancière's account of a poetics of the police qua decorum because it is exactly the capacity to coordinate the relation of fit between action and character along a sequential axis that enables him to claim that mimesis is not just a principle of resemblance but a normative theory for the codification and distribution of energies and labors along a dividing line of continuity that determines the distinction between good and senseless (or idle) work.[27]

In light of this, let me now briefly turn to Ricoeur's very helpful account of Aristotelian emplotment in *Time and Narrative*, volume 1. Doing so will allow us to better appreciate Rancière's sense of the relation between mimesis and decorum. Ricoeur begins by carefully and meticulously distending the "dynamic aspect" of "the art of composition" that he distinguishes from the "parts of the poem."[28] The emphasis here is on the activity of composition and design that he reads in Aristotle's articulation of mimesis and that he wants to distinguish from a more static sense of composition that could be (mistakenly) attributed to Aristotle's work.[29] "The essential thing," Ricoeur affirms, "is that the poet — whether narrator or dramatist — be a 'maker of plots' (51b27)."[30] And in making plots, the poet crafts an ethos. The *Poetics* gives priority to action, and in doing so it makes narrative action a conduit for ethical character.[31] The dynamism of human character is evident when the experience of crafted action activates understanding in the reader via interpretation. And all this is possible because there exists a "paradigm of order" that is also "a question of a kind of intelligence."[32] In short, Aristotle's poetics enlists a politics of fit by appealing to the dynamism of understanding as the human activity par excellence. On this rendering Aristotle convenes three distinct criteria — intelligibility, appropriateness, and fit — so as to generate a sense of necessity through co-herence. In this way emplotment offers the imitation not merely of right action but also of right fit.[33]

It is the coordination of the forces of fit, arrangement, decorum, and action in the *Poetics* that Rancière will read as Aristotle's prescription of decorum, as when he says that Aristotle's system of mimesis is "a generic principle that distributes modes of imitation as a function of the dignity of their subjects."[34] In the *Poetics* Aristotle outlines the imperative that any community of parts whatsoever (identified as singular substances or essences) must be arranged according to the necessity of purposeful action, thereby establishing right disposition as the only criterion for re-lating parts in a collective arrangement. This is Aristotle's theory of sense and understanding at the heart of his theory of emplotment. Another way of stating this is that by superimposing Aristotle's *Poetics* upon his *Meta-physics* we are given an isomorphic theory of solidarity where necessity is the principal qualification for inclusion, fit, and sense. That which is not necessary cannot belong because it lacks both sense and purpose: it is pure dissensus. In short, Aristotle's account of decorum determines an account of political belonging based on a theory of meaning.

Rancière's sensibilities will attend to how Aristotle's poetics of emplot-ment look, sound, and feel like a police poetics. This is because Aristotle's emphasis on the purposiveness of action is intimately bound to the cre-ation of an ecology of property and propriety that allots (i.e., emplots) per-sons and things to spaces and times. Rancière will therefore claim:

> The principle regulating the external delimitation of a well-founded do-main of imitations is thus at the same time a normative principle of inclusion. It develops into forms of normativity that define the condi-tions according to which imitations can be recognized as exclusively belonging to an art and assessed within this framework, as good or bad, adequate or inadequate. . . . I call this regime poetic in the sense that it identifies the arts — what the Classical Age would later call the "fine arts" — within a classification of ways of doing and making, and it con-sequently defines proper ways of doing and making as well as means of assessing imitations. I call it representative insofar as it is the notion of representation or mimesis that organizes these ways of doing, making, seeing, and judging.[35]

Rancière will also say:

> The police is not a social function but a symbolic constitution of the social. The essence of the police is neither repression nor even control over the living. Its essence is a certain manner of partitioning the sensible. We will call "partition of the sensible" a general law that defines the forms of part-taking by first defining the modes of perception in which they are inscribed. The partition of the sensible is the cutting-up of the world and of "world"; it is the nemeïn upon which the nomoi of the community are founded. This partition should be understood in the double sense of the word: on the one hand, that which separates and excludes; on the other, that which allows participation. A partition of the sensible refers to the manner in which a relation between a shared "common" [un commun partagé] and the distribution of exclusive parts is determined through the sensible. This latter form of distribution, in turn, itself presupposes a partition between what is visible and what is not, of what can be heard from the inaudible.[36]

Reading such passages in conjunction with our reconstruction of a poetics of mimesis allows us to appreciate the full force of Rancière's re-imagining of the police as something other than an authoritative and hierarchical apparatus of power. Instead he will rely on the sense of Aristotle I've outlined to articulate an account of police as a *dispositif*, a complex network of circulation enabled by the proper coordination of composite features that guarantee the right action in the right place at the right time. Such a coordinated composite of movement ensures maximum flow and maximum efficiency, like a traffic system designed to minimize gridlock. Hence Rancière's reimagining, in his *Ten Theses on Politics*, of the figure of the police as the traffic cop whose job it is not to halt the flow of movement (i.e., Althusser's "Hey, you there!") but to lubricate movement as much as possible so that agents are discouraged to stop and see (i.e., "Move along, there is nothing to see here"). Halting flow is precisely what the police want to avoid, on Rancière's rendering. And this avoidance is enabled and emboldened by a mimetic system committed to what William Connolly has recently articulated as a politics of "efficient causality."[37] In short, Rancière's ultimate concern isn't the coercive authority of police power that interferes with our freedom to act; his concern, rather, is with the dynamic power of a complex system of distributions that guarantees our freedom to act and move about freely and, in doing so, enables a specific form for act-ing and doing; that is, an isomorphic partition of the sensible.

Police thus refers neither to a system of oppression nor to a specific office or institution of control. Rather it is the name Rancière will give to a system of organization of life according to set principles of correspon-dence that operate in such a way as to govern the movement and flow of energies. Police is a regulatory principle for the distribution of sense and sensibility. And it works by conditioning those relations that count and those that do not count as appropriate fit. That "general law that defines the forms of part-taking by first defining the modes of perception in which they are inscribed" is made possible, indeed legitimated by an originary poetic gesture that establishes the rule(s) by which sensibility and fit are coordinated. This is the poetic *arche* that is also the metaphysical *arche* of Aristotelian mimesis that structures Rancière's poetics of the police.

PART 2: *Fabula Rasa*, or, the Contrarian's Fable

One central way we can appreciate the simultaneity of aesthetics and poli-tics in Rancière's thinking is to consider the centrality and dominance of an Aristotelian police poetics in our commitments to intelligibility and under-standing in political theory, in our accounts of what political action looks like, and in our investments in sense-making as a condition of political interlocution and participation. In the end Aristotle gives us an image of what good sense looks and feels like through his poetics of composition. And to the extent that the project of the *Poetics* is to persuade the reader to imitate good action, that work (and its ambitions) will look like a kind of aesthetico-political guidebook for a regime of politics committed to the primacy of representation; to wit, a police poetics. Political intervention and resistance will thus also be aesthetic, and these activities will involve a thwarting of Aristotle's "fable," as Rancière elaborates in the prologue to his *Film Fables*. Commenting on a passage by a young Jean Epstein written in 1921, Rancière says this: "Cinema discards the infantile expectation for the end of the tale, with its marriage and numerous children. But, more impor-tantly, it discards the 'fable' in the Aristotelian sense: the arrangement of necessary and verisimilar actions that lead the characters from fortune to misfortune, or vice versa, through the careful construction of the intrigue [*noeud*] and denouement."[38] It's not clear that this could count as an adequate account of cinema or, for that matter, of Epstein's sense of cinema. But it is, I believe, a good account of the kind of aesthetico-political intervention Rancière imagines when he speaks of the dissensus of partager. For what partager does is reorder sights and actions in such a way as to raze the dominance of representation as an epistemic demand, an aesthetic ambition, and a political necessity.

Consider, in this regard, *The Names of History*, which deals with the following historiographical problem: What happens to the science and writing of history when the conceits of its dominant poetic form have been undone by historical events? Situated at the beginning of the modern period, and contemporaneous with modern debates in historiography, *The Names of History* begins the critical work of problematizing the prevalence of Aristotelian *muthos* as the dominant style for the writing of history, and thus the dominant form of what Rancière will call "the poetics of knowledge." (Another way of stating this is to say that a central theme in *The Names of History* is to show how the democratic revolutions of the eighteenth century thwarted the Aristotelian fable, razing its dominance as the form of decorous action, and thus proliferating forms available to perception, sensibility, and action.)

A central scene that foregrounds the book's problematic is the explosion of papered words and the complications that such a dispersal procures. What the modern period enacts is "a revolution of paperwork in which royal legitimacy and the principle of political legitimacy find themselves defeated, fragmented in the multiplication of speech and speakers who come to enact another legitimacy—the fantastical legitimacy that has arisen between the lines of ancient history and of biblical writing."[39] The term *paperwork* is Rancière's way of registering a certain proliferation of acts of writing, transcribing, and registering that occurs when all of a sudden, and out of nowhere, many more people begin to count as agents whose tasks and capacities and doings demand documentation. Thus the development of technologies of certification and registration—of documenting as a political episteme and of documents as papered epistemic objects.[40] In short, one of the characteristics of the modern period that distinguishes it from previous historical times is the emergence of distorting genres of writing that challenge the privilege of the poetic regime of the sensible. Put differently still, a characteristic of the modern period is the disenfranchising of words from their proper fit and order in such a way that the Aristotelian fable is razed. It is as a result of this gesture, which involves multiple and plural activities of repartitioning of words and fit, that royal legitimacies "find themselves defeated." Such aesthetic genres, which Rancière identifies with the term *literarity*, "disrupt the relation between an order of discourse and its social function. That is, *literarity* refers at once to the excess of words available in relation to the thing named; to that excess relating to the requirements of the production of life, and finally, to the excess of words vis-à-vis the modes of communication that function to legitimate 'the proper' itself."[41]

More than a historical break or evental exception, Rancière here marks the revolutionary movements of the modern period as occasions for the thwarting of propriety and coherence through the illegitimate occupation of activities and practices that generate an excess of gestures and genres. The scenography of modern revolutions is, to invoke Ann Blair's helpful formulation, a scene of "information overload" characterized by a mélange of literary styles, aesthetic forms, and referential distortions.[42] The modern period inaugurates an unweaving of reference: "The ailment of politics is first the ailment of words," Rancière will assert while characterizing the Hobbesian position.[43] And this unweaving of reference enables illegitimate admixtures of terms. In short, for Rancière the modern period is characterized by aesthetic practices of mixing, collage, or montage that thwart the ambitions of a police poetics to determine the right disposition of things. Thus to identify any one form of subjectivity or agency as necessary to revolutionary politics is impossible because modern revolutions have undone the regime of mimesis that would have rendered identification possible.

Actually, that's not quite right. It's not that modern revolutions have undone mimesis, because mimesis persists. It is the case that modern revolutions have introduced the problem of illegitimacy of speech and action that can't be done away with by an appeal to right fit (i.e., decorum). This arises because of an eruption of the commons that evacuates authority and "provokes the proliferation of excessive speech."[44] Let's follow this thread: what Rancière identifies in *The Names of History* is the fact that historiography had to come to terms with the proliferation of new agents, new forms of agencies, and new capacities that multiplied the moment when kings, queens, and noblemen were no longer the titular agents of history's mimetic function: "The death of the king signifies that kings are dead as centers and forces of history."[45] The regicide that augurs the excess of words marks, for Rancière, a dissensus of decorum via a dissensus of mimesis. Aristotle had taught that good stories were those that included proper agents who performed necessary actions. He had also taught that there was a hylomorphic relation between good works and good character, and that right fit and proper correspondence guaranteed the existence of story rather than mere episodes. But all of a sudden the episodic overturns the epic; there are only bits of stories, minor events, the fluttering of shuffling paperwork. Anyone and anything occupies the space of the dead king; any episode can take the place of an epic; and the opposition between legitimate and illegitimate speakers is undone. In other words, what Rancière marks as the problem of historiography in the modern period is the collapse of the political status of epic action and the emergence of common practices by a common people who have no title, and thus don't count, as titular agents of history. More to the point, this rise of the commons happens without a common measure to collate this dispersal as an "in-common"; the only marker that the commons has is its vitalism as "the disturbance of the paperwork of the poor, this disturbance that invades lost time and puts history outside truth."[46] The commons is not determined by a signatory act of coordinated wills and negotiated principles of agreement (something Rancière will identify in *Disagreement* as a police force of consensus); the commons is, rather, the incipience of occupancy by intermedial entities whose capacities have no standing and who exist in between established forms of articulation — radical mediators, if you will, of scenographic transformation.

The political revolution of the modern period is thus also an aesthetic revolution. Aesthetics and politics both contribute to the razing of distinctions between subjectivities, activities, and their relations. "Such is the art of the aesthetic age," Rancière declares.

> It is an art that comes afterward and undoes the links of representative art, either by thwarting the logic of arranged incidents through the becoming-passive of writing, or by refiguring old poems and paintings. This work presupposes all past art to be available and open to being retread, reviewed, repainted or rewritten at will. It presupposes also that anything and everything in the world is available to art. Banal objects, a flake peeling from a wall, an illustration from an ad campaign, are all

available to art in their double resource: as hieroglyphs ciphering an age of the world, a society, a history, and, inversely, as pure presences, as naked realities brought to light by the new-found splendor of the insignificant.[47]

The aesthetic regime of art thwarts the representative regime by no longer making it possible to lean on reliable forms of correspondence between legitimate and illegitimate occupations and actions, just as it thwarts the political regime of representation that expects political action to fit the genre of the epic:[48] no action, and therefore no agent, is in principle illegitimate precisely because legitimacy as a criteria of value is put under duress. (This is what he means when, in the passage from *The Names of History* quoted earlier, he says that "royal legitimacy" is defeated by "a revolution of paperwork.") Thus neither image nor word can be said to represent anything, not because there is no referent in place but because there are too many referents, too many images, too many objects, too many words: the rise of the commons means a supernumerary occupation of all things excessive of any legitimate mode of counting. In short, aesthetics displaces representation. Hence anything and everything is available to art because art can no longer claim a specific function or a specific task. After the revolutions of the modern period, it is no longer the function or task of art to represent an external world. Rather the advent of the aesthetic regime of the sensible makes dissonance a practice of world-making.[49]

PART 3: To Band Apart

Rancière gives historical specificity to the razing of the Aristotelian fable in the popular revolutions of the modern period and the rise of excess as a specific concern for both politics and aesthetics. But given that this razing of fable is a constant in much of his writing about aesthetics and politics, one should not isolate this as a specific historical event. On the contrary, one might begin to appreciate this razing as characteristic, for Rancière, of a certain kind of modernism that goes by the name of "the aesthetic regime of the sensible." Indeed much of Rancière's more recent work, culminating with *Aisthesis: Scenes from the Aesthetic Regime of Art*, involves an exploration of the dynamics, technologies, practices, and particularities of forms of the razing of representation that coincide in peculiar ways with demotic moments of modernist aesthetic practices, literature and cinema chief among these.

As Hassan Melehy notes, "The fable of cinema, by its nature involving the unruly expressivity of the image, also thwarts the fable as a pure disposition of narrative events."[50] This, not because cinema offers a more accurate realism via its photographic transcription of reality or, for that matter, better stories. Rather what cinema does for Rancière is emancipate movement through automaticity because the camera has no fable to recount "but simply records the infinity of movements that gives rise to a drama one hundred times more intense than all dramatic reversals of fortune."[51] Automated recording thwarts Aristotelian emplotment by displacing the function of necessity in movement itself.

The immediate objection to such an insight will be to say something like "But surely this is false because in any scene there is an auteur or director managing the camera and arranging the shots, and so of course there is necessity and intention." But we know this objection can't be right because any director or cinematographer who shoots (or has shot) with celluloid film will rehearse without reserve the anxieties of filming a scene and having to wait for the next day's dailies. No matter what level of organization and control a director puts in place, no matter what technical level of expertise in lighting and framing a cinematographer may have, the fable will be generated automatically.[52] This is because the camera is an inhuman recorder that captures infinitesimal movements, colors, and contrasts that human eyes can't grasp. These are dimensions of experience that exist prior to their being qualified and plotted as useful or purposeful actions — notably the kind of work that happens after shooting, in the editing room. "This is why," Rancière concludes, paraphrasing Eisenstein, "the art of moving images can overthrow the old Aristotelian hierarchy that privileged *muthos* — the coherence of the plot — and devalued *opsis* — the spectacle's sensible effects."[53]

This is a demanding claim that assumes a great deal. Rancière is not shy about making such claims, but he is shy about explaining them. That's simply his style. (More on Rancière's style in chapter 3.) To appreciate the force of the claim, it is necessary to consider a potentially formative period of Rancière's cinephilic autodidacticism: French cinema of the 1950s. This was an especially influential period for the aesthetics of cinema in general, but also for the political history of film. It was a time when the intellectual testimonies of new writer-directors eventually identified with French New Wave cinema were debated and played out in the pages of the journal *Cahiers du Cinéma*. Crucial to these writings, and to the films made by the writer-directors, were the ideas elaborated on the role of editing as a creative process that does a certain kind of work of solidarity building. The aesthetico-political project was this: the conjoining of scenes and the establishment of nontraditional cuts, or montage editing, works to generate emergent relations not reducible to isomorphic forms of belonging. The site of aesthetic, political, and philosophical attention is on the dark precursor in between shots, which is the spatiotemporal domain where Aristotle had inserted the forces of necessity and probability in order to protect plot from the episodic and guarantee a sensible and decorous story. But the auteurs of the period refused the truism that editing meant continuity. Instead they played with the idea that a scene is not cut so as to repeat and confirm a preexisting sense of coherence; each cut invents a disjunctive relation between different shots. This is the philosophical claim made by Godard's jump-cut montage. But it is also a political claim that denies the existence of necessary relations. In short, cinema has the potential to raze the Aristotelian fable.

Consider, as an inroad into this insight, François Truffaut's "A Certain Tendency of the French Cinema," originally published in volume 31 (1954) of *Cahiers du Cinéma* that polemically pits what he calls "the Tradition of Quality" against the "*auteurs* who often write their dialogue and some of them themselves invent the stories they direct."[54] By the "Tradition of Quality" Truffaut means those films that, since the postwar period, had populated the screens of France and the film festivals of Europe under the banner of the tricolor. Truffaut names the perpetrators of this tradition of quality (Jean Aurenche and Pierre Bost especially), and he names their films. But more important, he names what he defines as the overarching political dilemma that drives the tradition of quality — and that dilemma is the technique of adaptation. The great tradition of quality, Truffaut states, doesn't make cinema but adapts novels to scripts and screen, and adaptation is equivalent to the negation of cinema. Thus he asserts, "Aurenche and Bost are essentially literary men and I reproach them here for being contemptuous of the cinema by underestimating it."[55]

Already we begin to see Truffaut's polemic pushing up against an Aristotelian commitment to imitation, for adaptation is imitation variously conceived. And imitation exists in tandem to what Truffaut calls "equivalence" that is at once a political and aesthetic failure.[56] Equivalence is an aesthetic failure because it denies the possibility of creativity due to the expectation that cinema remain faithful to the literary; it is a political failure for almost the same reason: because equivalence reduces all possible relations to one of fidelity to the repetition of a quality. That is, the enterprise of the tradition of quality (a nom de plume for "bourgeois decorum" if ever there was one), with its ontological commitment to the primacy of equivalence, denies cinema its transformative possibilities: "It is not an exaggeration to say," Truffaut declares, "that the hundred-odd French films made each year tell the same story."[57] He wishes to counter this metaphysics of mimesis with the kinds of artistic experiments he sees in the auteur filmmakers of his time (Renoir, Cocteau, Bresson, and Tati chief among them). The distinguishing feature of these auteurs is their willingness to push the technical limits of the art of cinema in storytelling, direction, *and* editing. The challenge Truffaut poses, in other words, is nothing less than a revolutionary overthrow of one system of artistic production (an Aristotelian one) for another (that of avant-garde auteur cinema) because, as he quips, "I do not believe in the peaceful coexistence of the 'Tradition of Quality' and an '*auteur's* cinema.'"

Truffaut's manifesto explicitly calls for an experimentation with the technical features of an artistic medium so as to alter and transform political relations. And this is because the ways of thinking about the relation of literature and film repeat and reproduce the isomorphic-mimetic relations of society. More than a claim about ideological subjectification, Truffaut's is an ontological claim about the entanglement of politics, aesthetics, and participation; the belief is that by exploring the technical limits of a medium one might transform social relations by distending the mimetic power of equivalence. Relations are not inalterable forms, and cinema is the technical medium that will allow Truffaut, Godard, and other New Wave directors to explore and exploit the possibility of thinking political and aesthetic intermediariness beyond the relation of mimesis prescribed by Aristotelian poetics.

These concerns find further expression in the debates between Jean-

Luc Godard and André Bazin regarding the value of montage. In a series of three short essays published between 1950 and 1955 and collected under the title "The Evolution of the Language of Cinema," Bazin praises the virtues of depth-of-field shots (a.k.a. long shots) over montage editing because the long shot allows objects and characters to be "relating in such a fashion that it is impossible for the spectator to miss the significance of the scene."[58] And the significance of the scene, Bazin explains, is its ability to generate a "unity of image in space and time."[59] For Bazin depth-of-field shots are contrasted to the reigning dialectical montage techniques of his day precisely because montage, as he says, "rules out ambiguity of expression," whereas the realism of the depth-of-field shot reintroduces "the uncertainty in which we find ourselves."[60] With specific reference to the Italian neorealist films of Rossellini and de Sica, Bazin will state that they "transfer to the screen the *continuum* of reality."[61] Depth of field wins out over montage as an aesthetic achievement, in other words, because it denies the possibility of grasping an already existing actuality by inserting the viewer into the everyday reality of movement (i.e., "continuum") and uncertainty. The style of montage that he criticizes — the dialectical montage most vividly associated with the Soviet school of Eisenstein — rules out ambiguity because it works to produce an ideal through the dialectical resolution of a contradiction: two contrasting shots, set up side by side in a montage editing sequence, will resolve into what Eisenstein calls a "gradational unity" that produces an ideal image.[62] And this dialectical resolution toward an ideal image is precisely why Bazin claims that ambiguity is ruled out in montage editing.

In his turn, Godard is dissatisfied with the idea that the creative practice of editing is simply reducible to continuity editing. Responding to what he likely perceived as Bazin's challenge to filmmaking, Godard will pluralize the capacities of montage and develop a mode of editing that refuses the idealism implicit in Bazin's account of its limits. We might say that whereas for Bazin realism was a style that put on display ambiguity and movement, cinema techniques like depth of field and montage quickly became rigidly designated practices that corresponded to specific aesthetic and political meanings.[63] Godard refuses this dividing line, and in "Montage My Fine Care" (originally published as "Montage, mon beau souci" in *Cahiers du Cinéma* 65, December 1956) he will unapologetically declare, "Invention and improvisation takes place in front of the moviola just as much as it does on the set. Cutting a camera movement in four may prove more effective than keeping it as a shot. An exchange of glances, to revert to our previous example, can only be expressed with the sufficient force — when necessary — by editing."[64]

Such an affirmation, subsequently put on display in his jump-cut edited driving sequences in *À bout de souffle* (1960), commit him to a different orientation than the one expressed by Bazin. The force of aesthetic achievement lies in the possibility of invention and improvisation, which is not reducible to any specific cinematic capacity. In other words, the practices of cinema are not fixed, and neither is the capacity of the filmmaker. She can be a director as much as an editor, an actor, a writer, or a stylist. The creative assembly of worlds that cinema puts on display is untethered to any specific sense of work or technical expertise or way of doing. Thus when Godard concludes his retort to Bazin by saying that "a director should closely supervise the editing of his films" and "the editor should also forsake the smell of glue and celluloid for the heat of the arc-lamps,"[65] what he is affirming is the fact that relations are not natural to any expertise, style, or capacity. But more than this he is affirming, through both text and cinematic works, that the lines of relation that establish divisions of labor, of practice, and of identity are not natural to any system of organization. Relationality, pace Bazin, is an incipient force that has no isomorphic necessity.

"To wonder whether cinema exists only as a set of irreducible gaps between things that have the same name without being members of a single body."[66] This formulation, found in the preface to Rancière's *The Intervals of Cinema*, expresses his commitment to the ideas formulated above: namely that cinema is an art of solidarity "where the old standards of representation for distinguishing the fine arts from the mechanical arts and setting everything in its place no longer exist."[67] We have seen a version of this formulation in Rancière's discussion of the unholding of mimesis in the age of the commons. The dissolution of the proper inaugurated by the age of modern revolutions created a space of indistinction where, to paraphrase Jacotot, everything is in everything, where words and vistas "occupy the terrain without designating any distinct social reality."[68] In cinema the occupation of excess is taken up by the dark spaces in between shots, the dividing line of the cut or — to use the technical term — the gutter in between each frame of film.

Walter Murch gives us a helpful description of this materiality when he asserts that film is cut twenty-four frames every second, each frame being a displacement of the previous one.[69] And Godard gives Rancière a compelling instance of this in *Histoire(s) du cinema* (episode 4A), when he (Godard) dissolves a montage of gestures and images and then lays them out in their bare particularity and simplicity.[70] The composite body of a shot is exposed, and the excessive minutiae of the movements stand in a becoming-relation to one another. Here a resonant adjacency (discussed in chapter 1) is put in full view. "Separating the images from their narrative arrangement is only the first part of Godard's project," Rancière explains. "The second, and more important part, entails transforming their nature as images."[71] By exposing the blackness of the cut he is offering an emancipation of visible movement that has immediate effects on the ambitions of intelligibility. That is, we cannot come up with good reasons as to why these cuts were assembled as they were. Their intelligibility is unverifiable because there is no common ground for their being together. Each shot is a no-part, a dislocated episode. A solidarity of parts emerges from the supernumerary excess of a dividing line that can no longer hold things in their right place. And with this experience comes a new form of dissensual solidarity, the solidarity of scene without the progress of time as its common measure.

Cinema is a technical medium capable of displacing the hierarchy of ordered plots, and hence the privilege of decorum, as a prerequisite of aesthetics and politics. But it is one among many such media. Indeed, as *The Names of History* makes clear, the challenge for politics isn't simply to establish a new order after the collapse of a preceding arche but to struggle with the presumption that the establishment of order is necessary to politics as such. And as Rancière shows throughout his oeuvre, this is as much an aesthetic problem as it is a political one. Indeed one of the reasons aesthetics and politics are indistinguishable is because both are milieus for the thwarting of a specific ideal of power that grants authority to a sense of inequality defined as the right disposition of things. As we saw in chapter 1, the problem for Rancière isn't so much to alter the structure of relations in any existing order but to render those forms of connectivity as parts of a collective ensemble open to dissolution and rearrangement. This, in the end, is one of the things cinema can do: to band apart vistas. "The literary, the cinematic and the theatrical thus come to seem not the specific qualities of different arts but aesthetic forms, relationships between the power of words and that of the visible, between the sequences of stories and the movement of bodies, that cross the frontiers assigned to the arts."[72]

And this achievement, if we can call it such, helps redefine modern politics. Politics can no longer rely on an account of action able to delineate a specifiable link between person and deed, just as history can no longer guarantee the epic as its specific genre, and film can no longer rely on continuity editing to generate an ideal image. In each case the compellant force of *necessitas non habet legem* (necessity has no law) is no longer sufficient.[73] There are too many actors, too many actions, and too many genres. To the list of aesthetic forms that thwart the relationship between sounds and vistas we must thus also add democracy itself as that form that traverses any specific norm of social and political coordination. From the perspective of Rancière's aesthetics of politics, democracy is the force of occupation of a commons without a common measure.

CHAPTER THREE

Rancière's Style

IN CHAPTER 2 I addressed Rancière's focus on decorum as a sentimental account of aesthetic and political isomorphism, his poetics of the police. I identified this as a force that circumscribes political participation and agency by confining what counts as relevant action and by whom. For Rancière this dynamic is situated first and foremost in the historical priority given to the Aristotelian fable and its formal account of fit and sequence, or mimesis and muthos. The metaphysics of emplotment drawn from the superimposition of Aristotle's *Poetics* and *Metaphysics* that is the basis for our modern notions of decorum and its implicit mimetic isomorphism make it so that only a specific class of people are entitled to perform good deeds.[1] Decorum's privilege is to allot value to action and designate who the doer of those deeds ought to be and what his or her stature is. Rancière introduces *partager* as a transformative mode of aesthetic mediation that occupies the dividing lines of a police poetics and rearranges the conditions of perceptibility and capacitation, thereby irrupting the catalogue of capacities for an affective pragmatics of aesthetics and politics.

Importantly, it's not that such rearrangements provide greater political access for marginalized groups; instead they make the question of access to political institutions irrelevant by detaching participation from qualification and judgment. Indeed it is the lack of qualification that defines the subjectivity of the agents' doing, hence the no-part as an intermedial and improper force of radical mediation.[2] As I noted with the examples of paperwork and montage from Rancière's writings in *The Names of History* and *Film Fables*, such capacities of transformation are not reducible to the willfulness of a political subject but rather result from an entanglement of human and nonhuman participants in diverse capacitational collectives.

In this chapter I shift emphasis from representing Rancière's overall ambitions and focus instead on his deployment and articulation of style in his writings. It is in his style of writing, and in his commitment to style, that one has access to Rancière's specific mode of occupation, the occupation of the page. As I show in this chapter and the next, his works are populated with objects and agents whose doings undo hierarchies and whose activities quite literally occupy him and his works. In short, in this and the subsequent chapter I put on display Rancière's own practices of aesthetic and political dissensus.

As noted, style counts as a particular activity of sentimental scenography that Rancière deploys for polemical purposes. As we also saw, analytic argumentation is not his preferred mode of theoretical exposition or genre of writing. He does not partake in the philosophical enterprise of conceptual clarification for the purposes of procuring sense and understanding. His resistance to the idea of proper fit between words and meaning makes that genre of writing unavailable to him. Instead he writes polemically in order to occupy his works with what he refers to as "the incommensurability of wrong, which alone establishes the body politic as antagonism between parts of the community."[3] What I show in this chapter, then, is how Rancière deploys style in order to capacitate a polemical mood that occupies his writings. I track Rancière's own writerly experimentations in literarity.

For Rancière style is best addressed by looking at the historical development of literature, specifically the rise and development of the modern novel. Why the novel? For two basic reasons: (1) It is in the novel that Rancière isolates that literary voice called *style indirect libre* that, as I noted, is for him *the* literary voice of equality. *Style indirect libre* offers visibility to anything whatsoever, thereby canceling the opposition between legitimate and illegitimate speakers, making it a radically egalitarian democratic style. (2) The novel emerges contemporaneously with the modern democratic revolutions and collaborates in what Rancière imagines as their shared amorphous form: each iteration of a novel is in excess of any formal definition of what a novel must be, just like each iteration of a *demos* is in excess of any general definition of a people.[4] In brief, both the novel and democracy are incipient forms of collective formation (i.e., the novel collects words; democracy collects persons) whose explicit manifestations either in print or in institutional founding are moments for the *in*-formation of a commons.

I pursue these lines of exploration for both diagnostic and corrective purposes. Though Rancière's writings have enjoyed increased reception and engagement in Anglo-American political theory circles in the past three decades, few readers have paused to ask what readerly dispositions are available to political theory other than an analytic framework that aims at outlining Porphyrian lines of argument. The de facto position approaches Rancière's writings, and his theoretical elaborations, with the assumption that one knows how to read, coupled with the intuition that an analytic eye will fund insights into the Porphyrian armature of his theoretical interventions. Such a stance is, however, counterintuitive not only to Rancière's sentiments as I have explored them thus far but also to his style of writing, which, as Bruno Bosteels rightly notes, "displays a brilliant use of the free indirect style of speech."[5]

To adopt *style indirect libre* as a style of theoretical writing and reading is not a fanciful choice for Rancière; it is a political and aesthetic choice.[6] And not to acknowledge *style indirect libre* as a significant dimension of his theoretical outlook is, I believe, to mute his words and to disregard the role that the practice of literarity plays in his own writings. For one element of Rancière's style is to develop his insights not simply through content but also through form. By this I mean that Rancière develops his insights through practices of composition and juxtaposition (literary and otherwise) alongside the exposition of a semantics of meaning. This is how his critical project appeals to one's sensibilities and challenges the divisions that distinguish sensation and understanding. But even more than this, acknowledging Rancière's adoption of *style indirect libre* allows us to better appreciate the principal role he gives to Flaubert's literary project for his own aesthetics of politics, a project that enables Rancière's reworking of Marx's critique of capital in the face of, and against, scientific Marxism.

I proceed by discussing Rancière's style as I see it playing itself out in some of his work, especially in the polemical title of his most commonly read work among English-speaking political theorists, *Disagreement: Politics and Philosophy*. I begin by tracing what I intuit to be Rancière's Marxist roots (and routes) in Marx's elaboration of capital's logic of equivalence. I then examine the central role *Madame Bovary* plays in Rancière's critical project, and I conclude by suggesting that we would be well served to move beyond the inherited orthodoxy of reading for argument so as to be more attentive to the critical potential in stylistics, not only in Rancière's oeuvre but also in the writerly stylings of other political thinkers.

PART 1: Polemical Sentiments

Rancière repeatedly notes the extent to which politics in the modern period is a matter of counting. The part of those who have no-part are unaccounted for, and thus disregarded as agents of politics. In a world where the science of politics is actuarial, the force of political change for Rancière comes from the supernumerary element of excess that is uncountable, that cannot belong to the set of participants who compose the collective whole of any specific social order. And as I've noted, one of the central features of Rancière's aesthetics and politics is to show that no representation suffices in containing all that may be accountable in its field of relevance, that there is always something more that can't be accommodated by any specific system of data analytics regardless of how big the data set may be. In emphasizing this supernumerary condition of accountability, Rancière is proclaiming the polemical *wrong* of the actuarial sciences of politics that privilege processes of justification as the basis of political legitimacy. (Here justification and legitimacy are technical capacities of accounting for what is right.) In its stead Rancière will attend to the processes of intraconnectivity of persons, places, and things. Hence the figure of Aristotle as an archetype in Rancière's oeuvre: Aristotle does not represent for Rancière the political philosopher par excellence whose ideas must be engaged, analyzed, and elaborated; he is, rather, the archetype of a sensibility, a disposition of critical thinking that implicitly partitions what is and what is not doable and thinkable. And in this, mimesis becomes the archetypal medium of an actuarial sensibility oriented toward policing the set of relations for politics that do or do not count. Aristotle is, of course, not unique in this role as a *dispositif* of political thinking. In distinct ways all of Rancière's writerly figures (Plato, Althusser, Flaubert, Jacotot, Marx, etc.) are formal figures who arrange sensibilities through their writings and through the morphology of their ideas, and Rancière's own practice of writing does the same. All these figures (Rancière included) are stylists of thought and action because their practice of writing is scenographic in that it involves the arrangement of words and ideas on a page, in the same way that painting is the arrangement of colors and geometric shapes on the surface of a canvas and filmmaking regards the arrangement of shots and scenes, lighting and color hues.

Hence Rancière's perspicuous attending to the arrangement of things, and specifically to the viscosity of spatialities and temporalities, visibilities and sayabilities, of persons, places, and events. With the sensitivity of the intuitionist, Rancière elaborates how any arrangement marks an ensemble of frictions that cannot be explained by expert knowledge. Arrangements are always up for grabs to the extent that their composite features remain indistinct from one another. These are the sentiments I have been exploring thus far in Rancière's oeuvre, and, I want to suggest, these are the sensibilities Rancière develops and adopts from Marx's analysis of capital's exchange logic. Mathematical sets presume the interchangeability (and hence equivalency) of parts. Qualities are known and fixed, and one part is as good as another, as in Marx's formula for exchange: "20 yards of linen = 1 coat, or: 20 yards of linen are worth 1 coat. The whole mystery of the form of value lies hidden in this simple form."[7] The whole mystery of the form of value, in other words, lies in a representational logic of equivalence that takes one part as exchangeable with another. The logic of equivalence, which we saw challenged by Truffaut's attack on adaptation in the "Tradition of Quality," admits the universal circulation of things: its ontology is flow, like the smooth flow of traffic that moves us along. Indeed for Rancière the logic of equivalence is the logic of the police, whose singular and solitary role is not merely to exercise power but to enable flow—the flow of signification among meanings, letters, and words. The logic of equivalence *is* the logic of the hermeneut's formula that says *x* must mean *y*, that 20 yards of linen represents 1 coat.

What Rancière gets from Marx is the sense that our theories of accountability—of making things count—are the basis of our science of politics and that actuarial science, whose job it is to predict a trajectory of equivalency through time, structures our logic of representation. This is Rancière's indelible picture of the police. The only way to break with this logic is to be wrong—to be unaccounted for. To be wrong does not mean to be incorrect. By *wrong* Rancière intends participating in the occupation of improprieties: if I do not count, if I am designated as a miscount by a logic of equivalence that relates only that which is in-common, then I will partake in a manner of equality that is—by definition—incommensurable because my part is extraneous to any orthodoxy of legitimation. The injunction to partake by the no-part is a polemical assertion of equality that cannot be defended. And it cannot be defended because it occupies and dissonates criteria of validation for mounting a justification. It may not be my place to be, to speak, to act, to read, or to write in this way, but I will do it anyway. To partake is to occupy that which does not belong: not in a sense of stealing but in a sense of occupying one's unbelongingness to a logic of equivalence that fluidly substitutes 1 coat for 20 yards of linen (and vice versa).

What Marx animates in Rancière's work is the intelligence of equivalency as capital's criterion for belonging to a part. A few words, then, about this word *intelligence*. It is, for Rancière, a term of art and not a measureable quantity like an IQ. By this I mean that intelligence is not something you possess but a qualification to which you may or may not have access. And the problem of equality lies in the criteria of eligibility for accessing intelligence: an intelligence is a regime of perceptibility that renders intelligibilities apparent, thereby awarding them the status of import. In this way it is not simply the intelligence of equivalency that is given priority in the critical theories challenged by Rancière but also the function of equivalency because the determination and designation of a common measure for thinking (which is what the intelligence of equivalency does best) is nothing other than the standardization of a common sense for thought. The value of 20 kilos of flax seeds, for instance, is not worth knowing unless they participate in an equivalency that renders 1 coat or 20 yards of linen. Rancière's point, which he inherits from Marx, is that the intelligence of equivalency is inegalitarian: "This supposed equality between cause and effect is itself based upon an inegalitarian principle: it is based on the privilege that the schoolmaster grants himself—knowledge of the 'right' distance and ways to abolish it."[8] Updated for today's late capitalist, neoliberal world, the assertion transforms itself thus: consensus is the logic of equivalency that is the intelligence of the police.

Notably Rancière's Marx is no longer a Marx who speaks for the poor or the proletariat. This he makes clear in the "Ten Theses on Politics" when he asserts, "There is politics as long as 'the people' is not identified with the race or a population, inasmuch as the poor are not equated with a particular disadvantaged sector, and as long as the proletariat is not a group of industrial workers, etc. . . . Rather, there is politics inasmuch as 'the people' refers to subjects inscribed as a supplement to the count of the parts of society, a specific figure of 'the part of those who have no-part.' Whether this part exists is *the* political issue and it is the object of political litigation."[9] What Marx gives Rancière is not a fetishization of the proletariat as a universal category for struggle. Rather Marx is the critical *dispositif* who renders a supernumerary unaccountability political. Marx's project is thus understood by Rancière as a project of acknowledging the supernumerary. Specifically Marx is the thinker who reconfigured human effort in industrial societies as labor, this in a time and in a world accustomed to conceiving of work exclusively in terms of agrarian or artisanal effort. In the closed loop of equivalence that discounts a worker's industry when fabricating coats or making of twenty yards of linen, Marx wants to render human labor perceptible as a social and political category, thereby making industrialized labor at once visible and sayable. Hence the adoption of the term *proletariat*, a word that hadn't been seen or heard since Roman classical antiquity that marks a formal category of inequality and unrepresentability. The ancient term referred to a class of people whose social contribution was simply that of biological reproduction and nothing else. The *proles* were a legal category of Roman citizenry who were so poor they could not serve the state by contributing money but only by contributing children. The adoption of the term to refer to nineteenth-century industrial workers articulates a formal class of persons who are so unaccountable that their only value is their capacity to exert physical energy for the reproduction of capital's goods.

Marx's theory of exchange relations and the efficient fluidity of substitution that the equivalency affirms also marks the crux of Rancière's critique of consensus. This is Rancière's polemical paradox because it is, in and of itself, a formula of equivalency that goes something like this: 20 yards of linen = 1 coat = equivalence = consensus. Rather than a principle of equality and inclusion, consensus is the name Rancière gives to the intelligence that governs the ensemble of relations in late capitalist society. In this he is unequivocal: "Consensus thinking conveniently represents what it calls 'exclusion' in the simple relationship between an inside and an outside. But what is at stake under the name of exclusion is not being-outside. It is the mode of division according to which an inside and an outside can be joined. It is the very invisibility of the partition, the effacing of any marks that might allow the relationship between community and noncommunity to be argued about within some political mechanism of subjectification."[10] What the intelligence of equivalence that goes by the name of consensus thinking does so well is lubricate the friction of a partition in such a way that inside and outside slide smoothly between each other and with viscosity. For consensus thinking *exclusion* is not a term that designates an externality; it is an operation that erases the difference between inside and outside, between community and noncommunity, so that there is nothing to dispute. Consensus renders the partition of exclusion invisible by qualifying democracy as the intelligence of equivalence; it terminates the polemical wrong of politics.

Rendering friction sensible is the work of the polemical wrong of dissensus that stages a conflict between two intelligences: the intelligence of equivalency and the intelligence of equality. This is the reveal in the title of Rancière's *Disagreement: Politics and Philosophy.* The title matters to me, as does the cover design by the University of Minnesota Press. The first thing to note about the title is that it is a good translation, but an inadequate one. The original French is *La mésentente*, which better translates as "the misunderstanding" (or even "a missed listening," as the root *entente* means both "understanding" and "listening") and has resonant adjacencies with having "bad blood" between people, especially between family members. A *mésentente* describes a family feud: a family dissemblance, if you will. This is decidedly not a disagreement because a disagreement is something you can (typically) resolve (e.g., with empirical evidence) or disregard (e.g., "Let's agree to disagree").[11] A disagreement implies an agreement on the terms of disagreement themselves, and a disposition of politesse too. Disagreements for Rancière are always politic but rarely (if ever) political. I can disagree with someone by contradicting her, though we both share a topic or idea in common about which we disagree. But I cannot misunderstand someone by contradicting her. A *mésentente* is not a contradiction but a "*missed* understanding"; it is a dissonance of consensus, or dissensus. And this dissonance is captured exceedingly well by the otherwise unexciting green cover of the Minnesota University Press publication that shows a light green inequality symbol ($\neq$) as a watermark on the darker green cover. That symbol, I would suggest, is a better translation of *mésentente* than the word *disagreement* that appears next to it because the mathematical inequality symbol marks the crossing out of equivalence that is the polemical staging of a conflict between two intelligences that plays itself out in that work and in Rancière's aesthetic and political writings more generally. There is thus a family dissemblance between politics and philosophy, which is the fundamental *mésentente* of democracy. What this means, finally, is that *la mésentente* and its corollary, dissensus, is not a concept for the understanding: it is, rather, an aesthetic practice of politics that disarticulates the conditions of sensibility for understanding. *Mésentente* is a sensibility.

Rancière's critique of the intelligence of equivalency must also be considered with the French notion of consensus in mind, a notion not reducible to a deliberative agreement between contracting parties, as is the case with the Anglo-American usage of the term. Whenever we English readers read *consensus* in the work of a contemporary French author, we must keep in mind that the corresponding French term is more likely than not *le bon sens*, the "good sense" of a *sensus communis*, which is at once normatively good and good common sense (e.g., as in the sensible of mimetic isomorphism).[12] *Le bon sens* is thus the good meaning that carries both aesthetic and political implications for Rancière.

This is a subtlety that can't quickly be discounted: the French critique of consensus does not register the term *consensus* as a deliberative agreement that may be attained given the proper conditions of intersubjective exchange. As I have already indicated, Rancière's title *Disagreement: Politics and Philosophy* stages a polemical dissensus that won't be resolved in the manner in which one might resolve a disagreement; the missed understanding ($\neq$) between politics and philosophy regards a dissensus of manners and sensibilities, and style, that can't be puzzled out by the faculty of the understanding. The *mésentente* of dissensus, in other words, marks the impossibility of arriving at a place of understanding that the politesse of good sense wants. What the polemical dissensus thus puts on display is the no-part of understanding (i.e., an ignorance) such that politics and philosophy will never be able to commune with one another. Put differently, the *ensemble* of democracy dissonates the *entente* (understanding) of consensus such that consensus is not necessary for solidarity. Philosophy wants *le bon sens*—the common sense that is also the good sense, the proper sense, the sense of propriety that comes with politesse—for under-standing. But Rancière's style of impropriety divines a mode of participa-tion in a commons "without a common measurement."[13]

Now it is imperative for the characterization I offer of Rancière's style that he never makes the points I raise explicit in his writings, though they occupy his pages throughout as formal features; his debt to Marx's elabo-ration of an intelligence of equivalency, for instance, remains unremarked, though it is palpably there. Hence my provocation that when reading Ran-cière we must attend to his words with the intuition of the sensitive rather than the analytic eye of the understanding. Rancière's *style indirect libre* solicits this, as is evident in his treatment of Flaubert.

PART 2: Inverting Flaubert's Legacy

The appearance of Flaubert in Rancière's pantheon of aesthetico-political *dispositifs* may strike some readers as odd or even gratuitous. Why Flau-bert? And isn't the choice of Flaubert the epitome of a kind of bourgeois elitism on Rancière's part? These are the kinds of questions that Rancière's polemical deployment of Flaubert beg for and that he addresses in a char-acteristically contrarian way. Within the sociology of the modern French philosophical canon, Flaubert stands as an important case study for the relationship between aesthetics and politics. This is because he is most fa-mous for the adoption and perfection of a formal literary style known as *style indirect libre*. And such an objectifying voice, as Georg Lukács, Jean-Paul Sartre, and Pierre Bourdieu all note, allows the author to take a distant stance vis-à-vis the social settings he is describing, especially in his mag-num opus, *Madame Bovary*. This is subsequently articulated as the epitome of a kind of bourgeois aestheticism that, as Bourdieu condemns, "tends towards a sort of moral neutralism, which is not far from an ethical nihil-ism."[14] No less a condemnation comes from Sartre, who describes Flau-bert's literary gesture as a petrification of everyday life that does away with people and things.[15] In short, within the French canon Flaubert's philo-sophical status is that of the unrepentant realist who crystallizes everyday living into a reified object of representation.

The figure of Flaubert is also important for the history of the rise of the novel as an artistic form and, as Frances Ferguson has shown, of the rise of literary criticism as a profession on par with medicine and the law. In her

chapter "Emma, or Happiness (or Sex Work)" from *Pornography, the Theory*
Ferguson traces the literary implications of the obscenity trial that followed
the serial publication of *Madame Bovary* (1856). The novel first appeared
as serialized episodes in the *Revue de Paris* (between October 1, 1856, and
December 15, 1856), and its publication in that forum caused a scandal.
It was deemed immoral, especially given the kinds of choices Emma, the
novel's protagonist, made, and, more explicitly, due to the graphic representations of Emma's extramarital affairs. The condemnation of obscenity
raised the matter of deliberating on the work's influence — to wit, can the
novel and the behavior of its protagonists be responsible for actions outside
the confines of its own pages? Famously the defendants of the trial (including Flaubert, his publisher, and the printer of the *Revue de Paris*) resisted
the obscenity accusation by declaring that the novel on its own, without
external support, accomplishes what the aspirations of the trial wanted to
accomplish, namely the condemnation of Emma's behavior. This is secured
by the fact that Emma kills herself at the end. The work could stand on its
own without requiring an external source of moral legitimacy that would
validate its status. In other words, the work was an autonomous object, despite the fact that it appeared as a feuilleton. The surprising result, as the
case history shows, is that the trial's judge agreed with Flaubert's defense,
and his agreement amounted to a kind of aesthetic judgment on the status
of the work of art: "The judge essentially affirmed that the novel had developed such internal consistency that no one would take its words as if they
meant what they might outside of its pages."[16]

This is relevant to our current concerns for several reasons. The first regards Ferguson's implicit ambition to show how literary criticism as a profession dedicated to the aesthetic engagement with literary works emerges
out of (or in collaboration with) legal judgment. That is, the standing of
a work as an aesthetic success or failure remains undecided among critics until it is decided by a judge. Ferguson's book is, in fact, a study in
legal case histories (of works deemed pornographic) that tells the history
of the development and gradual professionalization of literary criticism in
the modern period, alongside a series of intellectual and institutional de-
velopments that come with utilitarianism. In recounting this case history
of the emergence of literary criticism, Ferguson points to something that
(as I have suggested throughout) is a constant concern for Rancière: despite our admired distinction between reflective and determinative judg-

ment, the fact of the matter is that in order for a judgment (even of taste) to have purchase, it must perform as if it were a determinative (regulative) judgment. This is what criticism is: the transformation of a reflective experience into an authoritative determination. In the extreme cases of the obscenity trials Ferguson studies, the courtroom judge determines the standard of taste, and though this determination may remain contested in some circles, it holds sway in many others—most notably in those circles that embrace the development of aesthetic (literary) criticism as a profession. In other words, aesthetic judgment works as a judgment because it takes on the authority of a legal decision. And though this may not be the case in all instances of an aesthetic judgment (i.e., not all instances of aesthetic judgment are contested in courtrooms, nor do they require a trial judge to decide upon them), all instances of aesthetic judgment are determinative at the instant of their iteration, that is, at the moment of criticism. All of this to say that there is a substantive distinction to be made between aesthetic experience and the judgment that arises from it, and this distinction is something that matters to Rancière.[17] Hence his commitment (as he notes in the preface to *The Method of Equality*) to distinguish the function of the critic from that of the spectator who iterates a judgment and that of a participant in the articulation of a scene.[18]

The second reason Flaubert is so central to Rancière's oeuvre regards the status of the novel as a work of art. In our day and age this issue is difficult to fathom given that the novel's standing as a potential contender for artwork is rarely in question. But if we enter into the perceptual sensibilities of a nineteenth-century Parisian readership we might begin to have a sense of the culture wars occurring in the period. Consider two images: a page of the first edition of Baudelaire's *Les fleurs du mal* (1857; figure 3.1) and two pages of the first edition of *Madame Bovary* (figure 3.2).

The difference between the two volumes is striking. Not because of their content, which is an obvious difference; not even because of the different literary forms, though that is more relevant for the matter at hand. But for the manner in which the forms of the respective genres (poetry and novel) are displayed. The visual difference between the two works is in the population of words on the page; to adapt Rancière's terminology, an excess of words occupies the page of the novel in a way that can't happen on the page of the book of poetry. The words on the pages of Baudelaire's volume look sparse, deliberate, poised. Those of Flaubert's tome are populous,

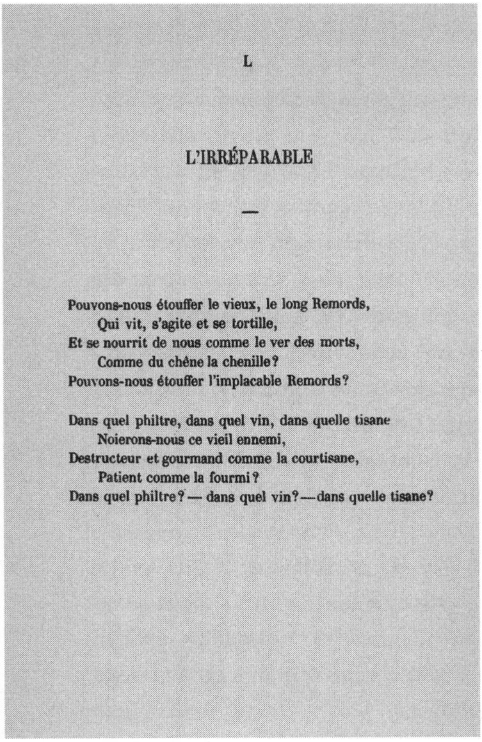

L'IRRÉPARABLE

—

Pouvons-nous étouffer le vieux, le long Remords,
  Qui vit, s'agite et se tortille,
Et se nourrit de nous comme le ver des morts,
  Comme du chêne la chenille?
Pouvons-nous étouffer l'implacable Remords?

Dans quel philtre, dans quel vin, dans quelle tisane
  Noierons-nous ce vieil ennemi,
Destructeur et gourmand comme la courtisane,
  Patient comme la fourmi?
Dans quel philtre? — dans quel vin? —dans quelle tisane?

FIG. 3.1 — A page of Charles Baudelaire, *Les fleurs du mal*, 1st ed., 1857. Scan by author.

FIG. 3.2 — A page spread of Gustave Flaubert, *Madame Bovary*, 1st ed., 1856. Scan by author.

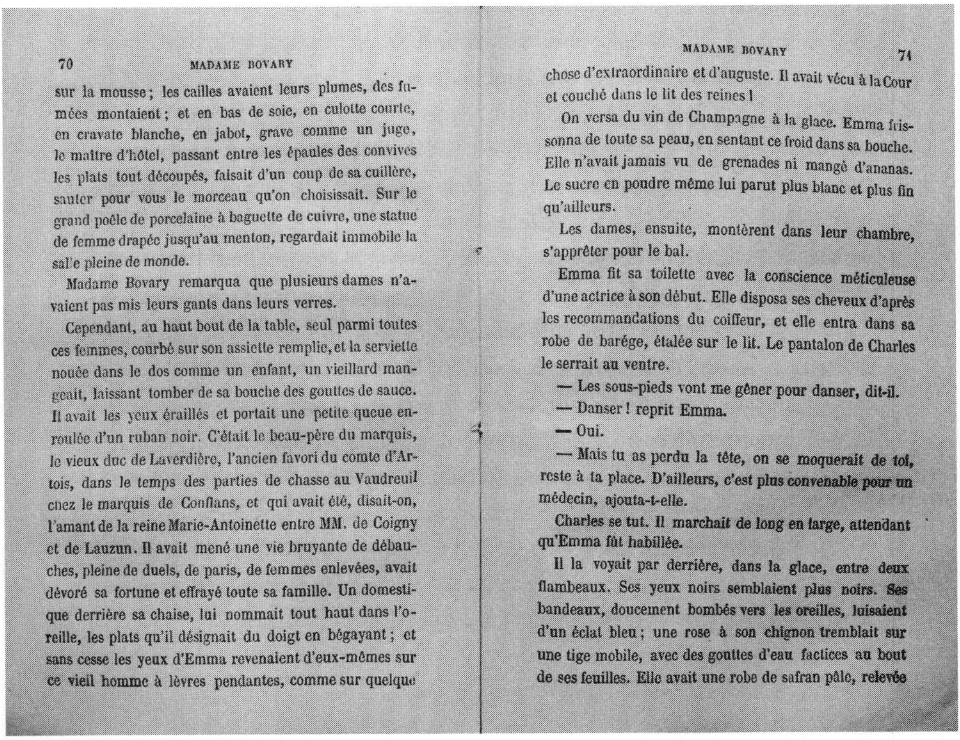

sur la mousse; les cailles avaient leurs plumes, des fumées montaient; et en bas de soie, en culotte courte, en cravate blanche, en jabot, grave comme un juge, le maître d'hôtel, passant entre les épaules des convives les plats tout découpés, faisait d'un coup de sa cuillère, sauter pour vous le morceau qu'on choisissait. Sur le grand poêle de porcelaine à baguette de cuivre, une statue de femme drapée jusqu'au menton, regardait immobile la salle pleine de monde.

Madame Bovary remarqua que plusieurs dames n'avaient pas mis leurs gants dans leurs verres.

Cependant, au haut bout de la table, seul parmi toutes ces femmes, courbé sur son assiette remplie, et la serviette nouée dans le dos comme un enfant, un vieillard mangeait, laissant tomber de sa bouche des gouttes de sauce. Il avait les yeux éraillés et portait une petite queue enroulée d'un ruban noir. C'était le beau-père du marquis, le vieux duc de Laverdière, l'ancien favori du comte d'Artois, dans le temps des parties de chasse au Vaudreuil chez le marquis de Conflans, et qui avait été, disait-on, l'amant de la reine Marie-Antoinette entre MM. de Coigny et de Lauzun. Il avait mené une vie bruyante de débauches, pleine de duels, de paris, de femmes enlevées, avait dévoré sa fortune et effrayé toute sa famille. Un domestique derrière sa chaise, lui nommait tout haut dans l'oreille, les plats qu'il désignait du doigt en bégayant; et sans cesse les yeux d'Emma revenaient d'eux-mêmes sur ce vieil homme à lèvres pendantes, comme sur quelque

chose d'extraordinaire et d'auguste. Il avait vécu à la Cour et couché dans le lit des reines!

On versa du vin de Champagne à la glace. Emma frissonna de toute sa peau, en sentant ce froid dans sa bouche. Elle n'avait jamais vu de grenades ni mangé d'ananas. Le sucre en poudre même lui parut plus blanc et plus fin qu'ailleurs.

Les dames, ensuite, montèrent dans leur chambre, s'apprêter pour le bal.

Emma fit sa toilette avec la conscience méticuleuse d'une actrice à son début. Elle disposa ses cheveux d'après les recommandations du coiffeur, et elle entra dans sa robe de barége, étalée sur le lit. Le pantalon de Charles le serrait au ventre.

— Les sous-pieds vont me gêner pour danser, dit-il.

— Danser! reprit Emma.

— Oui.

— Mais tu as perdu la tête, on se moquerait de toi, reste à ta place. D'ailleurs, c'est plus convenable pour un médecin, ajouta-t-elle.

Charles se tut. Il marchait de long en large, attendant qu'Emma fût habillée.

Il la voyait par derrière, dans la glace, entre deux flambeaux. Ses yeux noirs semblaient plus noirs. Ses bandeaux, doucement bombés vers les oreilles, luisaient d'un éclat bleu; une rose à son chignon tremblait sur une tige mobile, avec des gouttes d'eau factices au bout de ses feuilles. Elle avait une robe de safran pâle, relevée

dispersed, and require containment. The novel just looks busier, and each word feels as if it were a word in the crowd. That is, in the novel's layout the margins do the work of containment because the words feel as if they might flow off the page at any time. Hence the fear, on the part of Flaubert's obscenity prosecutors, that the novel's words might have effects outside its pages; hence also the significance of the judge's decision that the novel didn't need an external support such as an obscenity condemnation to determine what its effects might be. The novel could have its own support even though the words on the page are so amorphous and populous that it's difficult to fathom how they might be contained. The poem, on the other hand, is self-contained: its form is its integrity, and it doesn't require margins to do the work of containment. In short, the words on the page of a book of poetry seem to remain in place on their own (they are, to invoke a term from previous chapters, well disposed), whereas the words on the page of a novel risk spilling out along its edges if the margins are not properly set. From a purely visual perspective, the novel occupies the page with an excess of words in a manner that the formal requirements of the poem, at least in the nineteenth century, could not.

For Rancière the occupancy of an excess of words matters to his aesthetics and politics. The debate, and the contest, between the novel and poetry in the nineteenth century revolves around the standing of a made object as a work of art and what criteria one may point to in order to ascertain its completeness when the object in question is a perpetually incipient, constituent form that persistently eschews the availability of set genre conventions for deciding whether it is a complete work.[19] How can a novel be a work of art—a complete and integral work—when it looks as if the words would spill out along its edges if it didn't have an external support (such as pagination)? The crisis of literature in the nineteenth century, in other words, is a contest over the sufficiency of hierarchies of evaluation in the face of populous, amorphous forms. Like the excess of words that marks the popular democratic revolutions of the modern period, the novel is an incipient collective formation that populates and problematizes set genre criteria of the work of art. This is why Rancière turns to the novel, and especially to *Madame Bovary*, as an exemplary democratic aesthetic object— not because of its standards of taste but because of the amorphous nature of the medium itself and the work that the excess of words on the page do to our sense of democracy as an event of popular occupation.

To bring this issue into better focus, consider the debate on legal interpretation between Ronald Dworkin and Stanley Fish that began with Dworkin's essay "Law as Interpretation."[20] In that essay Dworkin analogizes the interpretation of the U.S. Constitution to the serial writing of a novel. He then claims that the first writer in the series of this imagined chain-writing exercise is less constrained than the next, and so on, all the way down the chain, so that the final author is most constrained because of the preceding history and the obligation to remain faithful to the storyline. Interpreting the Constitution (and hence the normative status of precedence) is like writing a novel in that it is an exercise in seriality and sequencing that demands a certain sense of continuity with what had been previously established, interpreted, and written. Dworkin is happy to call that sense of continuity a tradition of interpretation, or historical precedence.

In "Working on the Chain Gang" Fish retorts by insisting that Dworkin not only has a mistaken account of interpretation but that his mistaken account is rooted in a mistaken sense of the integrity of the novel.[21] What matters in the debate is how one understands the relationship between the episodic, its sequencing, and the status of completeness. For Dworkin, completeness is precedence, hence the possibility of claiming an increased burden of responsibility along the interpretive chain. For Fish, each instant of an iteration is a complete thing on its own and requires work so as to be connected to a previous or subsequent episode; whatever work is done in relating the two episodes, that relation is not natural but artificial because — and this is the Flaubertian point — no external source can guarantee completeness to a series. The novel's completeness, and thus its standing as a work, is as incipient as the demos.

Rancière notes that in the nineteenth century literature faced a crisis not unlike the crisis that marks the point of contention between Dworkin and Fish (my analogy, not his). The term *literature* began to shed its meaning as the expertise held by men of letters "and came to refer instead to the art of writing itself."[22] This development problematized the division of the Aristotelian and belletristic hierarchies that "tied the rationality of poetic fiction to a certain form of intelligibility of human action, to a certain kind of affinity between ways of being, ways of doing and ways of speaking."[23] In short, the novel introduces a crisis of representation that is at once a social, political, and aesthetic crisis. And Flaubert's novel and the trial that revolved around it, as well as its legal declaration that transformed the episodic work into a work of art, becomes a kind of ground zero for rethinking the relationship between aesthetics and politics. As Ferguson explains, Flaubert's novel was exonerated from any accusation of obscenity, whereas Baudelaire, also accused of obscenity, would be prosecuted only a few months later for *Les fleurs du mal*. The poet of nineteenth-century modernism created a work of poetry that could not stand scrutiny as a self-sustainable work of art in the manner in which Flaubert's episodic novel could, despite the fact that both works were deemed important works of literature.

And this is perhaps the point: what Rancière wants to chart with the contest of literature in the nineteenth century is a kind of razing of hierarchies that emerges at the moment when both *Les fleurs du mal* and *Madame Bovary* could stand as comparable works of art, so comparable in fact that both could be recognized as obscene works worthy of a legal trial. In raising this fact, and in affirming that "Flaubert made all words equal just as he suppressed any hierarchy between worthy subjects and unworthy subjects, between narration and description, foreground and background, and ultimately between men and things," Rancière returns us to the question of a politics of aesthetics that had seemed settled by Lukács, Sartre, and Bourdieu. In his now familiar contrarian and polemical sensibility, Rancière inverts these others' hierarchies. More than the archetypal author of the bourgeois novel, Flaubert is the person who contests an easy judgment about the aestheticization of politics as a project of bourgeois aestheticism because "the writer had to be wary of trying to prove anything. But this indifference to any message was, for Flaubert's critics, the very mark of democracy which, for them, meant the regime of generalized indifference, the equal possibility of being democratic, antidemocratic, or indifferent to democracy. Whatever Flaubert's feelings about the people and the Republic may have been, his prose was democratic. It was the very embodiment of democracy."[24]

Herein lies Rancière's challenge to Lukács, Sartre, and Bourdieu, a challenge that we have seen take shape elsewhere too. To consider aesthetics entangled with politics is not to assume that there is a politics to a work and to read or interpret a work as political based on criteria external to that work's conditions of production. The interpretive mores of Lukács, Sartre, and Bourdieu are the same mores that brought Flaubert to trial, though not the same mores that informed the judge's verdict. For those who accused Flaubert of obscenity, like those who accuse him of bourgeois aestheticism, did so not on the basis of the work itself but on the basis of its potential or possible effect, its presumed influence outside the bounds of pagination. Rancière, on the other hand, refuses to account for the aesthetic exclusively as a category of necessary effects consequent to the performance or iteration of a work or an action. Rather for him aesthetics is political because it is "a mode of intervention in the carving up of objects that form a common world."[25] And Flaubert accomplishes this carving up of objects (specifically that object called "literature") by giving priority to the absoluteness of style, not as a kind of haut-bourgeois aestheticism but as the "dissolution of all order. Raising style as an absolute meant firstly pulling down all the hierarchies that had governed the invention of subjects, the composition of action and the appropriateness of expression."[26] For Rancière, Flaubert's democratic style occupies literature by having words occupy a page and, in so doing, dissolves the aesthetic hierarchies that had guaranteed the political divisions of taste and that had identified literature exclusively with poetry.

PART 3: On Democratic Style

Rey Chow writes that Rancière's "good-humoredly ironic essay" on *Madame Bovary* sees the main character, Emma, as having contracted a kind of disease that condemns her to death.[27] Emma's predicament is that "of a common folk's way of pursuing democracy" by "turning her fleeting sensations of pleasures (culled from romance novels, natural and architectural surroundings, and other mundane associations) into real things and people to be desired and possessed"; these are "serially replaceable and substitutable" in such a way that Emma's predicament foreshadows the "high modernist principle of juxtaposition or collage."[28] So when Lauren Berlant, in recounting her debt to the literary critic Barbara Johnson's poetics of indirection, explains that *style indirect libre* "performs the impossibility of locating an observational intelligence in one or any body, and therefore forces the reader to transact a different, more open relation of unfolding to what she is reading, judging, being, and thinking she understands," she means that *style indirect libre* exacts the impossibility of determining an external authority that authorizes the necessity of any specific form of intelligibility or understanding.[29] With his adoption of a *style indirect libre* Flaubert managed to render the voice of the novel (the narrator's voice) so utterly impersonal that it was impossible to determine the nature of the subjectivity of whoever was speaking. Another way of stating this — the way that matters to Rancière — is that Flaubert managed to democratize prose by making it so that no one stature, status, qualification, or intelligence is necessary for accessing the work. That is, you do not have to know who the narrator is — or indeed who Flaubert is — in order to appreciate the novel. By rendering the narrator's voice as impersonal as any other ready-made object that went into the collage of elements that compose the episodic ensemble, Flaubert developed a new regime of the art of writing that "blurs the distinction between the world of art and the world of prosaic life by making any subject equivalent to any other."[30]

Such a disjunctive relation characterizes the force of indistinction in dissensus, a force that disarticulates the correspondences of equivalency that authorize partitions. Indistinction renders things impersonal by interrupting the authoritative categories we assume necessary for adjudicating their (our) distinctiveness.[31] Flaubert thus offers Rancière "a new form of indistinction," one that is captured by Flaubert's ambition of developing an "absolute way of seeing things": "The absolute way of seeing things is the way you see them, feel them, when you're no longer a private subject, pursuing individual ends. Things are then freed from all the ties that make them useful or desireable to us as objects. They deploy themselves in this way in a sensorium of pure sensations, detached from the sensorium of ordinary experience."[32] In short, the work of impersonality and indistinction is the work of aesthetic disinterest that liberates people and objects from the forces of necessity that arrange them according to a specific structure of correspondence and representation.[33] It is in this way, I would submit, that style matters to Rancière and that aesthetics is always political. It is always political because aesthetics is the force that thwarts procedures from the necessity of due process; aesthetic experience is the name we give to the forces that render necessity unnecessary.

For Rancière, then, Flaubert's *style indirect libre* does two important political things: it makes available the indistinction and impersonality of aesthetic experience, thus interrupting the intelligence of equivalency (e.g., if things are indistinct, they are not measureable and hence unavailable for an equation of equivalency); and it democratizes authority such that anyone or anything whatsoever can partake, just as anyone or anything whatsoever can count as the voice of the narrator in *Madame Bovary*. Here impersonality and indistinction are forces for an elision of identity as a condition of political participation. As we have seen, what matters most to Rancière is that there not be any necessary criteria for belonging to the category of a political subjectivity, and the forces of indistinction and impersonality denounce the availability of criteria tout court, thereby procuring a disordering of the proper (i.e., *arche*).[34] Here is Rancière on this point: "free indirect discourse used not to make one voice speak through another but to efface any trace of voice, the imperfect tense used not as a temporal marker of the past but as a modal suspension of the difference between reality and content of consciousness, fluctuation and the anamorphic value of pronouns ('he began rummaging . . . it [*elle*] had fallen . . .') or the function of an 'and' that isolates rather than coordinates."[35] And here he is again:

> When *Madame Bovary* was published, or *Sentimental Education*, these works were immediately perceived as "democracy in literature" despite Flaubert's aristocratic situation and political conformism. His very refusal to entrust literature with any message whatsoever was considered to be evidence of democratic equality. His adversaries claimed that he was democratic due to his decision to depict and portray instead of instruct. This equality of indifference is the result of a poetic bias: the equality of all subject matter is the negation of any relationship of necessity between a determined form and a determined content. Yet what is this indifference after all if not the very equality of everything that comes to pass on a written page, available as it is to everyone's eyes? This equality destroys all of the hierarchies of representation and also establishes a community of readers as a community without legitimacy, a community formed only by the random circulation of the written word.[36]

The mélange that composes an ensemble of indistinct parts that have no reason for belonging together other than the fact that they happen together is an archetype for the radical *an*-arche that is the aesthetic force of democracy. Democracy is aesthetic, in other words, because democracy is the name we give to an intensity of indistinction, impersonality, nonnecessity, or indifference; it is the name given to the forces of associations of persons, places, and things that do not make sense together as an ensemble.

Rancière's style thus puts on display that any arrangement is premised on a fundamental missed understanding, by which we can now entail an absence of the necessity for understanding. "This style," he affirms, "is not the sovereignty of one who manipulates sentences and forms, the manifestation of an individual's free will in the sense in which it is ordinarily understood. It is, on the contrary, a force of disindividualization. The power of the sentence is a capacity to manifest new forms of individuation."[37] The status of the sentence as an assembly of words is thus more than a meaningful utterance: it is a coordination of elements — a mélange of parts — that exists but not exclusively for the understanding. Politics is not a project of the understanding, and to the extent that philosophy desires understanding, it must remain tethered to the conditions of necessity that structure and arrange a poetics of the police.

In summary, the project of understanding is, for Rancière, the intellectual ambition of the social sciences and humanities that limits the possibility of ensemble. This is because the project of understanding presupposes a reliable sense (*le bon sens*) that affords given correspondences between object and meaning, and thus extant correspondences between criteria and works of art. In doing so it is not possible to create new forms of solidarity because for the understanding such assemblies are derived, not created, and they are derived from a necessary common measure that is the source of identification and collectivization. A *missed understanding* (*mésentente*), on the other hand, is concerned with thinking incipient forces of solidarity in a world where the smooth circulation of equivalency reigns. This also helps explain why democracy *is* dissensus for Rancière: democracy is the name given to forms of individuation that dissent from the given. In this regard Bruno Latour's reminder of the link between democracy and division is helpful: "The word 'demos' that makes half of the much vaunted word 'demo-cracy' is haunted by the demon, yes, the devil, because they share the same Indo-European root *da-* to divide."[38]

Coda: Amorphous Forms

Style diverts our readerly and intellectual efforts away from the project of the understanding as the sole and only mode of political theorizing. Rancière's critique of Althusser discussed in chapter 1 and his elaboration of the dissensus of politics as a fundamental missed understanding (*mésen-*

tente) is not only a polemical gesture against the authoritative voice of philosophy and its subjugating role in determining the nature of what can be known and how (e.g., method). It is also a claim about the nature of political criticism: critical thinking, for Rancière, does not require a specialized knowledge that unearths the contradictions of logic so that speech may be judged irrational. Quite the contrary, critical thinking is rooted in the sensitivity of the intuitionist who senses the ways in which authority can be disindividuated from a specific form. To reduce critical thinking to the science of epistemology—as the Aristotle-Althusser critical *dispositifs* do—is to incur tutelage in a model of authority that persistently conserves criteria. One can never partake in epistemological critical thinking; one can only reproduce it. This is because the intelligence of equivalence that structures such a model of critique remains transcendental and prior to one's enactment of it. Like poetry and the belletristic arts, political philosophy's commitment to a hierarchy of forms for political thinking institutes hierarchies of participation for the activity of political thinking. In contrast, Rancière considers democratic thought and action to be forms of innervation that occupy those interstitial chronotopias that hierarchies condemn.

Hence the archetypal stature of Flaubert and Rancière's contrarian reading of the novelist's and novel's democratic aspirations. Flaubert's prose is democratic precisely because *style indirect libre* liberates form from the necessity of having shape. While it is true that Jacotot offered a comparable remedy by making everything relevant to the classroom setting, that remedy was necessarily tethered to a specific scenario. Flaubert doesn't need that unique setting because he makes the indistinction of ignorance a condition of being in language, through style. In this respect we might consider *style indirect libre* an ignorant style that anyone can embody simply because it ignores qualifications for its own occupancy and deployment.

The proposal that I forward in this chapter is that rather than reading Rancière's theoretical writings for the purpose of conceptual clarification and analytic application (what Wolin famously calls the "appliances" approach to theorizing) we are best served by reading them through their stylistics, as "processes of connections . . . produced by a becoming of (their) terms."[39] What I have otherwise called a sentimental readerly mood is particularly relevant when reading Rancière's oeuvre, especially given his aesthetic and political commitments to radical equality and solidarity, as well as his deployment of *style indirect libre* that thwarts the decorous ambitions of a Porphyrian eye. My own practice of reading Rancière locates his work of political theorizing not in the content and meaning of his terms but in the form of his writing. There is no doubt that Rancière is a formalist, though his particular manner of formalism is immanent rather than transcendental.[40] He is taken by forms of amorphousness as they occupy diverse spaces, surfaces, and media. And he deploys these forms throughout his writings. In this chapter I focused on the amorphousness of the written word and its occupation on the page through Rancière's deployment of *style indirect libre* as both a mood and a manner of democratic indistinction. In the subsequent and final chapter I will look at amorphousness as a temporality of reverie.

CHAPTER FOUR

Rancière's Democratic Realism

THE AMBITION of this final chapter is to elucidate how amorphous form occupies temporalities as well as spatialities in Rancière's oeuvre. Rancière's account of emancipated participation imagines an unauthorized partaking of indistinct and interchangeable parts by anyone or anything whatsoever. Another way of stating this is that for Rancière, political action has an amorphous form. This is his realism. It is a realism that takes for actuality the fact that political action has no ideal content, shape, gait, or orbit, that anything can comingle with anything else, and that there are no relational forces preassigned to specific qualities of persons, of rank, and of things. Hence dissensus as a force of dissidence that dissents from the hierarchies of decorum's dispositional arrangements.[1] Such dissent is what Rancière understands by the terms *emancipation* and *equality*, which are per se not simply concepts and certainly not prescriptions; these are political relations that involve an improper — or unauthorized — partaking in/of something that the established hierarchies of a social order denies.

An example already visited is of those nineteenth-century workers recounted in *Proletarian Nights* who took the time of night as a time of leisure for writing rather than sleeping and recovering from the day's labors. Rancière shows that the workers reconfigured the night from a time of purposive restoration to one of unpurposive reverie. Such moments of unauthorized partaking are legion and "aim to create and recreate bonds between individuals, to give rise to new modes of confrontation and participation."[2] At stake in what Rancière otherwise describes as reality's "mixed character" is nothing less than the reunion of emancipation and dreaming that twentieth-century critical theory, especially in its critically denunciatory, high modernist, or scientific Marxist mode, did much to impugn.[3] Reappropriating the temporality of reverie — that is, partaking in what Rancière refers to, citing Rousseau's *Nouvelle Heloise*, as the "*farniente* of reverie"[4] — is the task of his democratic realism. The very possibility of supposing a world where words, phrases, vistas, and sounds do not belong together drives his democratic realism, a world, that is, where words, phrases, vistas, and sounds *do no-thing*—they don't even make sense. This "do no-thing" is quite literally the *farniente* of reverie that stands within Rancière's lexicology as the temporality of partaking by that interstitial force of radical mediation he calls "the part of those who have no-part."[5]

As we've seen throughout, when dealing with someone committed to distancing himself from the privilege of analytic arguments as the form of political theorizing, as in the case of Rancière's polemical contrarianism, it is important to note the extent to which the epistemic attitude and its expectations of decorum are consistently troubled. I've shown that one of the things at stake in Rancière's sentiments is a resistance, to the point of disregard or even rejection, of the sacrosanct epistemic-political relation. An implicit commitment in his aesthetics and politics is to emancipate political thinking from the *sensus communis* of the epistemic as *the form* of political theorizing in order to afford emancipatory politics the possibility of reverie. To enact such an affordance, Rancière turns to two important resources that, though distinct, are intimately related: (1) the literarity of *style indirect libre* as an amorphous form of democratic prose and (2) aesthetic realism. I discussed the first point in the previous chapter; in this chapter I'll focus on the latter. Some preliminary remarks, then, on this term *realism*.

For Rancière, realism is not representational, nor is it prescriptive. That is, his realism is not concerned with "the way the social, economic, political, etc., institutions actually operate in some society at some given time, and what really does move human beings to act in given circumstances," as Raymond Geuss would have it.[6] Crudely put, Rancière's democratic realism does not correspond to an actuality, either current or past. Rather it is a site of contest regarding the nature of the actual. Realism in this instance attends to the practices of ensemble formation, as well as to the ways arrangements of words and signification, of workers and sleep, of films and fables are untethered and disjoined. Such disjunctive relations exist in a state of perpetual unbelonging as the excessive element of any mélange resists the urge to consolidation. Here is Michel de Certeau explaining this point in a different, though related context: "Rather than representing a return to the real, 'realism' expresses the release of a population of words that until now had been attached to well-defined facts and that, from this point on, become useful for the production of legends or fictions."[7] Such emancipations from assigned relations and allotments motivate Rancière's sense of realism and its affective pragmatics.

Rancière's aesthetics of politics is committed to two fundamental and related goals: to develop a critical disposition not invested in the intelligibility of things and to develop a project of political participation committed to the aesthetic claim of disinterest.[8] To consider his aesthetics of politics is thus to think the possibility of an unpurposive politics of unintelligibility, where the critical task is, as counterintuitive as this may seem, to *not* understand. This is what he refers to as "a scandal in thinking proper to the exercise of politics."[9] Scandalous political thinking comes with the realization that understanding is not political and that there is a pluripotential domain of political action and experience — the amorphous domain of the *farniente* of reverie — where people and things do nothing. This is why, as I noted in chapter 3, the title of Rancière's book *La mésentente: Politique et philosophie* does not translate well as "Disagreement" but is better read as a treatise on misunderstanding or "missed understandings." To make misunderstanding central to political thinking through an interplay of aesthetic disinterest means refusing the social scientific and hermeneutic ideal that all labor, including intellectual labor, must be oriented to a specific instrumental ideal. Another way of stating this is that for Rancière, the category of ignorance does not indicate an intellectual deficit but instead an account of the nature of interplay.

In this final chapter I return to *Aisthesis*, and more specifically to the prelude and scene 14 entitled "The Cruel Radiance of What Is," so as to explore the dynamics of Rancière's democratic realism. Each of the scenes in that work displays a temporality of reverie as a scene of missed understanding, where something political is happening but where the faculty of understanding has no purchase on either justifying or legitimating the happening. In other words, the faculty of understanding is helpless in deter-mining the affective pragmatics of play developed in the scenes of *Aisthesis*. For here reverie is shown to be a kind of playful indulgence that rearranges conditions for relating to the world as it may have been previously con-ceived. Take Loïe Fuller's serpentine dance that, for Rancière, "illustrates a certain idea of the body and what makes for its aesthetic potential: the curved line."[10] The idea of the serpentine line had already been introduced in eighteenth-century England by Hogarth to challenge linear perspec-tive, or the line of sight of the representative regime of the sensible. And, as Rancière notes, Edmund Burke showed that the serpentine line stood for "the rejection of the classical model of beauty."[11] Fuller's dance ulti-mately gives the geometric line serpentine movement and puts on display its potential for "perpetual variation of the line whose accidents endlessly merge."[12] It's a kind of suspended animation, which, in the case of this spe-cific scene, is the nature of reverie's farniente.

I spend some time in this chapter reviewing the operation of emancipa-tion via indistinction and indifference discussed earlier in the book that I claim is at the heart of Rancière's democratic realism. The aesthetic prac-tices that procure indistinction blur the dividing lines that structure any social order, rendering them serpentine, if you will. In short, indistinction or indifference is the operation of curving that makes the realism of reverie possible. I then show the connection between realism and reverie at work in Rancière's oeuvre, where reverie is a state of temporal suspension that emerges from a condition of disinterest that itself arises out of the inability, in that moment and in that state of missed understandings, to attribute the qualification of interest to any one thing. A sensibility that runs throughout Rancière's oeuvre is thus the following: the realism of reverie emancipates action from purposiveness by insisting that action not be scripted. Thus it is not a matter of learning what action is but of occupying a suspended temporality in the everyday world of the farniente, which is not a utopia (or no-place) but a time that belongs to no one.

PART 1: An Affective Pragmatics of Disinterest

As we've seen, the police line is a dispositional arrangement that assumes an innate relation of cause and effect implicit in all actions and relations. It thus refers to two operations at the same time: the privileging of linearity as a mode of relating and the representation of all relations *as* linear. A crucial element of the police line is its ability to make participation purposive by requiring that action align with specific effects, that it be productive. If the only relations that count are causal and linear, then no form of participation can take place other than a purposive one. Or, better put, any other supplementary form of partaking is illegitimate. And so already we begin to see the extent to which, for Rancière, the police line is a sensibility of time and movement as well as order and arrangement. The police line administers the totality of relations and inclusions; it assigns movement and trajectory as well as orbit and influence. It is, in every sense of the word, a disposition intended to confine forms of participation.

Equality arises when necessity is rendered indistinct, that is, when the dividing line that distinguishes swerves. Hence democracy as that form of association crafting without qualifications. The assumption here is a sentimental one: pace Aristotle, the demos is not constituted on the basis of a natural relation that determines the conditions for community. On the contrary, the feature that enables the incipience of a demos is disinterest toward the necessity of any formal constituent arrangement. Without interest or qualification there can be no prescriptive force for the constitution of a collectivity because indifference "destroys all of the hierarchies of representation and also establishes a community of readers as a community without legitimacy, a community formed only by the random circulation of the written word."[13] Once we acknowledge the fact that relations are not innate or natural, the only thing left is to admit that anything can comingle with anything else, that no relation is illegitimate because legitimacy is not a quality of relationality. And this admission is the work of aesthetic experience that "frees the sensory events from the links of identity and usefulness."[14]

Let us pause for an example that Rancière's work invites, given what we have seen as his commitment to cinematic montage as an aestheticopolitical practice. "Godard," Rancière states, "clearly makes his point by dissociating things that are indissociable."[15] The phrase is ironic: How does one make a point by dissociating things? It is ironic also because the phrase points to a practice in Godard of dissociating the commonsense relation between image and plot in cinema. Consider in this regard Anna Karina's character Odile in Godard's caper classic *Bande à part*, who, when told it is time to plan the caper, breaks the fourth wall and turns to the camera (and audience) to ask "Un plan? Pourquoi?" (figure 4.1).

FIG. 4.1 — A scene from *Bande à part*, directed by Jean-Luc Godard, 1964. Screenshot from Criterion Collection DVD.

"A plan? What for?" This, as if to declare that the film itself has no plan but is simply a series of recorded movements and gestures assembled in a plan-like way. (*Plan* is the French word for the cinematic shot that, Ronald Bogue notes, "has its origin in the early silent cinema, when filmmakers spoke of establishing continuity between planes of action in succeeding scenes.")[16] Such moments of dissociative acknowledgment arrest because they render serpentine the elements of the film, elements that possess no inherent logic of movement and arrangement. The title of the film suggests this: *Band à part* (noun) refers to the trio that is the thieving collective, but *Band à part* (verb) also refers to the act of theft which is a loosening of binds (i.e., a banding apart) that displaces things from one place to another. The fact of association is not bound to a necessary logic or justification; participation is *un*reasonable, if you will. Hence the force of Godard's montage that "decomposes the assembly of gestures and images and returns them to their basic elements. The universality of his art is that it establishes the most basic elements, and assemblies thereof, that make a discourse and a practice intelligible by making them comparable to other discourses and practices, by, for instance, making a political discourse and union comparable to a declaration of love and a love affair."[17]

Rancière elicits other scenarios in *Aisthesis* to emphasize his practice of emancipation as the partaking of aesthetic indistinction. In reality, for him emancipation means blurring, "the blurring of the boundary between those who act and those who look; between individuals and members of a collective body."[18] Thus instead of answering the question of what is beautiful or what is art or what is useful in art for politics (all questions he is uninterested in answering), he occupies his works with minor scenes of aesthetic disinterest to underscore how aesthetic experience blurs the given relations within any existing configuration. And this occurs because aesthetic experience renders things indistinct from, indifferent to, or impersonal toward one another in the manner in which Godard will render indistinct, indifferent, or impersonal the relation of image and plot. These three terms — indistinct, indifferent, and impersonal — are used interchangeably by Rancière to designate the reality of nonnecessity; the reality that there is no proper to politics. We can thus begin to sense that his realism is a kind of thwarted realism because it is not invested in a fidelity of correspondence to an actual world but to the felt experience of a dissolution or betrayal of that correspondence.

PART 2: Reverie, or, the Time of Disinterest

Reverie is the suspended temporality of the measureless mélange, suspended in the sense that it has no definitive direction. It is at once impersonal and improper to the extent that within this mixed state the certainties of property and propriety do not hold. The idea of reverie is crucial to Rancière's elaboration of democratic politics not because reverie promises an emancipatory imaginary or a politics of the imagination. On the contrary, the state of reverie is the actual state of democracy — it is democracy's real, if you will — that is persistently threatened by diverse modes of denunciation that come in those authoritative judgments that affirm the perpetuity of partition. But the serpentine line generates a state of reverie, a state of animated suspension where things simply stop operating as they had as the result of the occupation of past practice by new forms of partaking. Reverie is thus the name Rancière gives to the time of unauthorized partaking in leisurely activities that generate a serpentine doing.

The discovery of the farniente of reverie requires Rancière to abandon the expectations of both explanation and prediction as viable modes of social science research. "To account for the subversive power of their work," he writes of the worker-poets, "I was forced to break with the habits of social science, for which these personal accounts, fictions, or discourses are no more than the confused products of a process that social science alone is in a position to understand. These words had to be removed from their status as evidence or symptoms of a social reality to show them as writing and thinking at work on the construction of a different social world."[19] The science of the social as the science of the purposive statement has no time for reverie. And yet here is an entire *an*-archive, a "heap of broken images" as Miriam Bratu Hansen calls it,[20] of political and aesthetic material that registers the unpurposive real of an assembly of participants whose activities are politically subversive not because of their outcomes but in and of themselves, as activities for the perpetual variation of the divisions of time and space. And they do so not as a result of a political program or on the basis of institutional requirements but simply because they are enacted.

There is thus no doubt that such moments occurred, and they are not an exception to the status quo, though they remain inexplicable to a common science of the understanding. But the problem is how to account for the lost time of reverie within a science of politics that articulates purposeful action as timeless deeds. What of those acts that are not deeds but that nonetheless mark a doing that is happening, even if that doing is no-thing? The task at hand for Rancière becomes one of abandoning a purposive social science and the actuarial ambitions of evidentiary accountability so as to give research space and textual time to the farniente of reverie.

The status of irrelevance attributed to unpurposive acts is a sustained site in Rancière's writings that allows him to affirm the realism of reverie for democratic politics. Such reverie, as I've suggested, is not the reverie of an imagination with a purpose but refers to activities without necessary or planned effects; it refers to a mode of action that is unusable and hence unprescribeable. In contrast to those modes of theoretical engagement that expect heroic virtue (and thus political relevance) of exceptional events in history, Rancière turns his political, aesthetic, and scholarly attention to everyday practices that are amorphous to the criteria of relevance. In doing so he puts pressure on the anxiety to specify the relevance of any one activity. In short, what Rancière's turn to the farniente of reverie points to is a refusal of those modes of critical judgment that easily assign qualifications of relevance to actions so as to determine the nature of right action for emancipatory politics. Like the aesthetic object that, on its own, is neither relevant nor irrelevant because its value is undeterminable, the activities of the farniente trouble, to the point of dissolving, the expectations of purpose. The result is a serpentine dissuasion of action from purpose that renders any action or activity whatsoever dissonant. The farniente of reverie thus restores the actuality of an accursed share of emancipatory politics.[21] But to accept this—that is, to accept reverie's farniente as a political temporality, and specifically as a transformative time—requires a troubling (for some) corollary: the unpurposiveness of reverie puts pressure on our inherited dogmatism about the centrality of judgment as a political faculty. For what the forces of measurelessness, unpurposiveness, indistinction, and reverie all point to is the refusal to privilege a theory of judgment as necessary to politics. Rancière's democratic realism involves a disregard for judgment since crucial to judgments are determinations that are unavailable in the measureless mélange of reverie's farniente.

PART 3: Rancière's Serpentine Scenographies

To be sure, Rancière does not affirm the irrelevance of judgment. There is no implied synonym between unpurposiveness and irrelevance. Rather the matter at hand is to show the transformative powers of aesthesis regardless of judgment's expectations and ambitions. It is with this emphasis on transformations in mind that we can begin to see how the project of *Aisthesis* is, as he says in the prelude to that book, a companion to *Proletarian Nights*. What do I mean by this? Simply put, in order to discard the model of judgment that Rancière identifies as the dogmatic drive of critique that emphasizes the right knowledge for politics and identifies a hierarchy of purposeful acts, he will have to introduce a series of literary and aesthetic substitutions that take the place of (in the sense of occupying the space of and thus taking the part of) the established epistemophilia. In *Aisthesis* he will thus explore fourteen scenes of sensorial transformation (properly put, these are instances of a demotic modernism) that exemplify the availability of an emancipated movement that "does not succeed in reintegrating the strategic patterns of causes and effects, ends and means."[22]

There are fourteen scenes in *Aisthesis*. Each is autonomous in relation to the others. And though they are laid out in chronological order, that chronology does not imply any kind of lexical priority or necessary rank. Each of the scenes, then, presents a passage in a work as a singular autonomous thing, an object with its own support. The scenes are arranged as indistinct to one another and thus are relatable to one another, though their manner of relating remains unassigned. The formal layout of *Aisthesis* is paratactic. It creates the opportunity of a serpentine line by insisting on the absence of a beginning, middle, or end. The book has a project, no doubt, but it doesn't have a plan (recall Odile: "Un plan? Pourquoi?"), and the reader is free to start at any point in the book and move about freely. *Aisthesis* is a book of aesthetic and political theory that, in composition and layout, comes perilously close to transcribing the aesthetic features of filmic montage.[23] It is a book with no depth, a glass surface. It is a work that at once announces the insufficiency of a hermeneutics of suspicion for political criticism, denies the strategic effectiveness of a symptomatic reading, and performs the sinewy movement of reverie's farniente it seeks to put on display. Given its subject matter, it is a book curiously devoid of judgments or explanations, despite the fact that it begins and ends with one great castigation: the denunciation of expert judgment via its denunciation of innate relations as embodied in the Marxist avant-garde ambition of "rigor" when analyzing capitalism and art, politics and aesthetics, avant-garde and kitsch.[24] But that denunciation is less a judgment than a polemical assertion of a wrong that queers the relationship between rigorous analysis and relevant evidence by introducing the idea that when all is said and done, anyone has the capacity to do no-thing. And *Aisthesis* will show us fourteen scenes of such good-for-no-thing-ness. Indeed the conceit of *Aisthesis* is that democracy itself is a practice of mediation that transforms the arrangements of the broken pieces or found objects he calls "the part of those who have no-part."

As there is no lexical priority, rhyme, or reason built into the exposition and elaboration of *Aisthesis*'s scenes, I will focus on the one that strikes me most vividly: scene 14, "The Cruel Radiance of What Is." The scene begins, as they all do, with a passage; this one is a partial description taken from James Agee and Walker Evans's *Let Us Now Praise Famous Men*. As with all the other scenes in the book, Rancière does not explain the words or the vistas he cites but lets them appear on their own so as to make available the transformations of the sensible fabric therein. His style favors description over explanation.

The Agee-Evans collaboration bespeaks a farniente at two levels: the first is the farniente of the image-text relation in journalism, and the second is the farniente of propriety of tone by, as Rancière says, seeming "to transpose Balzacian descriptions of bourgeois interiors to the setting of poor life."[25] The Agee-Evans collaboration began as an established genre with a mission: *Fortune* magazine, at the time specializing in long-form photojournalism, sent Agee to Alabama to document the lives of share-croppers during the height of the Dust Bowl, and Agee enlisted Evans's help. "But," Rancière notes, "the two friends soon took a decision that lent their cooperation unique allure: each one of them would work alone. Text and photographs would be independent. No photograph, indeed, would show the reader the cracks in the bureau or the family of china dogs. Photos would bear no captions. And no reporter's text would explain the circumstances in which the photographer gathered certain members of one of the three families."[26] Herein lies the crux of the farniente scene, its reconfiguration of the sensible: the scene marks a collaboration without union or unity wherein each participant (Agee and Evans) and each object (word and photo) is a do-nothing with the other. Like Winckelmann's Belvedere Torso, what we have here is a singular break with the representative regime through Agee and Evans's decision of having nothing to do (i.e., farniente) with one another. The effect is the creation of a scene where words have no-part with images, and images no-part with words, and each no-part does nothing. Words and images will thus operate as ready-mades in this scene of broken relations and reconfigured conventions. By deciding to band apart, Agee and Evans dance the serpentine line between journalism, photography, and realism. It is true that the representational regime in photojournalism would ask its practitioners to supplement words with images, and images with words, so as to present an accurate account. And no doubt this is what the *Fortune* editor expected of Agee: an accurate and unembellished narrative. After all, Agee was known for having written that kind of realism before. No one would have predicted that he and Evans would break with the expectations of mimesis, an expectation defined "by the champions of a certain modernism" that "opposes the carefully chosen elements of art to the vulgar inventories of 'universal reportage.'"[27]

And so we have a reconfiguration of (at least) two different sensorial plateaus: the transformation of the relation between word and image, which transforms (or dismisses) the necessity of each having to provide explanations of what there is to be seen and known; and the transformation of the expectations of representation itself that, like the Belvedere Torso, requires a reconfiguration of the hierarchies of criteria that assign the qualities of stature and decorum to objects. "The champions of a certain modernism," as Rancière identifies those judges without naming them, refers to that category of decorous criticism that presumes that the sensibility of taste possesses innate qualities. It is those same judges and critics who identify the coincidence of taste with rank, and judgment with capacity. But the reverie or interruption or blurring or dissensus — in short, the serpentine dance — that the Agee-Evans collaboration enacts dissonates the common measure that assures the equivalences which a certain modernism wishes to uphold. And the result? An indistinction of things, place, and order that ignores qualification by occupying the pages of their collaboration with an excess of the trivial — to wit, a demotic modernism. This is, ultimately, the power of a democratic realism that admits of the measurelessness of the mélange and thus of the insufficiency of sound judgment as a marker of social and political privilege and, especially, direction for action. Here is Rancière on Agee-Evans one final time:

> The "frivolous" or "pathological" count of singlets, clothespins, rusted nails, espadrille eyelets, broken buttons, and lone socks or gloves in the Gudger house is a way of making these objects useless for any account of the situation of poor farmers given to the — traditional, reformist or revolutionary — doctors of society. This is precisely, says Agee, the only *serious* attitude, the attitude of the gaze and speech that are not grounded on any authority and do not ground any; the entire state of consciousness that refuses specialization for itself and must also refuse every right to select what suits its point of view in the surroundings of the destitute sharecroppers, to concentrate instead on the essential fact that each one of these things is part of an existence that is entirely actual, inevitable, and unrepeatable. The "frivolous" inventory of the drawers only fully renders a minute portion of the elements that are gathered in the infinite and unrepeatable intertwining relations between human beings, an environment, events, and things that ends up in the actuality of these few lives.[28]

To acknowledge the actuality of these lives means having to embrace triviality and frivolousness, those markers of farniente that specialization at once refuses and denies. And this occurs in *Let Us Now Praise Famous Men* not simply at the level of presentation but also at the point when Agee and Evans's collaboration is enacted in the mode of the no-part ("each one would work alone"), enabling the photos to bear no caption and the words to bear no illustration. It is, like Flaubert's page, a collaboration without support, overpopulated by an excess of ornamental detail.[29] The result is a complete reconfiguration of the genre of journalism, and with it, a reconfiguration of how words and images can and may relate — that is, as indistinct to one another.

Only by appreciating the actuality of indistinction can we appreciate the force of Rancière's democratic realism. Through his scenographic practice of staging elements as indistinct from one another he is able to make explicit in the scenes he selects how the worlds depicted are sinewy inventories that bear the weight of the actual. The risk is to romanticize the poor, the downtrodden, the sharecroppers whose lives bespeak a "cruel radiance," and the consequence of this risk is to disregard them. Romanticization singles them out as a distinct lot whose places and times have been apportioned. But Rancière will refuse that strategy. For "the cruel radiance of what is" doesn't come from a celebration of the sharecropper's condition, as if the task is to single out the true hero of life's randomness. It is quite the opposite: the task of the scenography is to isolate the weight of an art of living that arises when the representational order of words and images can no longer bear the weight of common measure.

What Rancière wants to do with this scene isn't to celebrate the genius of two artists who accurately depict the suffering of others. On the contrary, he wants to attend to the aesthetic arrangements curated by the sharecroppers on their own terms and put on display how Agee and Evans's attention to such an ornamental aesthetics does not come from an indexical act of representation that wants to pinpoint a true reality. Rather, by denying journalism's genre convention of using images to supplement text and text to explain pictures Agee and Evans allow the fact of living to emerge from their elision of a "right disposition of things."[30] They distort the common conceit that the purpose of words and images is to explain reality.

In discussing Dziga Vertov in another of *Aisthesis*'s scenes, Rancière says this: "A film is not a matter of putting a story into images meant to move the hearts or to satisfy the artistic sense. It is primarily a thing, and a thing made with materials that are worthwhile on their own. This is the principle

Vertov adopts . . . only cinema of the fact."[31] This cinema of the fact is not a realist documentary. It is the realism of a doing no-thing, of rearranging things that are already there. "Vertov does not simply want to film facts. He wants to organize them into a film-thing that itself contributes to constructing the fact of the new life."[32] Something similar can be said (and will be said) of Agee and Evans as well as of Chaplin and Winckelmann and all the other scenographers in *Aisthesis*. Why scenes? And why this scenographic mélange? Simply put, *Aisthesis* puts on display, in both content and form, Rancière's democratic realism that centers on the fact of mediation in everyday life. Politics is participation in forms of doing against those acts of judgment that affirm the uselessness of the farniente. "How useless it is for sharecroppers to have decorations! Rather than dedicating their time and effort to ornament, they should spend their time working harder so they can lift themselves from their misery." And yet, Rancière wants to say, it is precisely in those micro moments of do-no-thing-ness that we uncover new worlds and novel forms of participation dissident from the common sense of decorum. Such serpentine acts construct the fact of new lives. In short, the realism of democratic reverie dissents from a mimetic realism that imagines the work of political thinking as the procedure of justification for the right disposition of things.

Throughout his career of writing and research on the aesthetics of politics one of the things that Rancière's explorations of the farniente of reverie make clear is that the expectation of the accountability of time is a constant site of political inequality. As we have seen throughout these pages the farniente of reverie is a time of leisure, a luxurious moment of the frivolous passing of time when minutes, if not hours, happen without scope or aim. Not just anyone is entitled to time's passing. Such leisurely luxuries are reserved for industrious people of any age whose heroic acts of bravery save the economy or make history. These *auctors* are the ones entitled to do nothing because their lives are otherwise occupied with purposeful, authoritative acts. Rancière's democratic realism disrupts this sensible fabric of temporal causes and effects, of means and ends, of acting as doing, in order to set the stage for a radically egalitarian democratic partaking. What the farniente of reverie does, in other words, is discharge action with the burden of having to matter, of having to achieve, of having to produce, so that any act whatsoever may have a radiance of what is.

CONCLUSION

Demotic Modernisms, Popular Occupations

RANCIÈRE'S SENTIMENTS explores the ways in which Jacques Rancière puts on display and into practice a radical mode of mediation whose operations transform the scenographies, perceptibilities, sensibilities — and thus the actual conditions — of worlds. This, and nothing less, is at stake in his aesthetics and politics. I explore this insight by structuring each chapter along a dividing line. Thus chapter 1 exploits the division between repetition and transformation in accounts of mediation; chapter 2's fulcrum lies between mimesis and aesthetics; chapter 3 pivots between the form-content axis; and chapter 4's division is between purposiveness and do-nothing-ness. All of these partitions are at once present and on display throughout Rancière's oeuvre, and they source occurrences of occupation by popular modes of radical mediation that displace the institutional isomorphism that perpetuates the existence of those very same divisions. Radical mediation, in other words, dissonates the police line.

None of the capacities that occupy Rancière's writings is an expert practice, nor are any of the moments of occupation themselves exceptional in the way the extraordinariness of the political exception has been imagined.[1] Rather, they are immanent moments of media play at once diurnal and popular, and though there is a technique to them, that technique is not specialized but that of the autodidact. It is a technique resonant with Roger

Caillois's classification of play as *paidia*, a participatory mode of interaction that emerges outside of the rules of a game, "an almost indivisible principle," Callois explains, "common to diversion, turbulence, free improvisation, and carefree gaiety."[2] In short, *paidia* describes the force of *partager* in the *farniente*. Those who partake of it are not entitled to have access to the rules of the game. It is thus in the very nature of partager to be a turbulent diversion. Rancière speaks of practices that transform sensibilities and that render vistas and soundscapes anew. This, among many other reasons, makes him a sensibility thinker and author. But more than this, his account of the transformations of sensibilities, and the forms of affective pragmatics that enable these, suggests that the work of aesthetics and politics is play and that play is a force immanent to the intermediacy of partager.

All of this to say that Rancière lives in a world where division and dissent are in constant play with one another. Partitions, distinctions, dissensions, and lines—these terms populate his writings and are iterated so as to put on display the repetition of divisiveness that coordinates contemporary political life. Althusser gives us epistemic breaks so as to establish a scientific theory of political critique in order to guarantee emancipation as an outcome. In doing so he arranges the proper disposition of knowledge in relation to authority so as to create a harmonious order of mind that may be deployed to overcome alienation. Rancière, for his part, occupies his texts with popular diversions that dissonate the epistemic ambitions of the expert. Hence the centrality of solidarity, emancipation, participation, and equality to his aesthetics of politics. The entirety of his thinking and writing is directed toward showing how divisive spaces and times, the lines of division that structure a partager, can be occupied and played with by popular forces immanent to the structures that generate those divisions. To *partager* in this sense is to handle something that does not belong to you, not for the sake of appropriating what is rightfully yours but for the sake of playing with it and diverting its world. Thus to Rousseau's founding gesture of inequality—"This is mine"—Rancière replies with an *ignorant gestu*: "This is not mine, but I will play regardless."[3]

For Rancière's aesthetics and politics, then, there can be no politics of belonging, whether ontological, existential, or proprietary. Belonging is of the order of the general, not the particular. This is also why it's not possible to reduce aesthetic and political agency in Rancière's oeuvre to a theory of the subject or a politics of recognition. A subject of politics always already exists as a subject of politics, regardless of whether or not that subject is recognized as a legitimate agent. Rancière's actants, however, are neither authorized actants nor acknowledged exclusions; they are nonsubjects with no relation to subjectivity. They are an ensemble of human, technical, singular, and plural forces that occupy the interstitial domains of divisions, those in-between spaces of mediation that constitute the dividing lines in any social field. And this ensemble, this collectivity, is incipient.

This suggests that in Rancière's account of an aesthetics of politics the reader will not find a theory for overcoming divisions. It is true that his sentiments are those of the contrarian who generates and occupies divisions and diversions. But such forms of occupancy are not tantamount to an overcoming of divisions. Divisions can't be overcome, in the same way that the geometry of the line can't be undone: a line can be made serpentine, it can be diverted, it may be dripped on a canvas rather than drawn with a ruler, but lines persist. This is to emphasize once again that Rancière's mode of mediation is not dialectical but transfigural. You don't overcome divisions because divisions are not contradictions you can explain away; you occupy partitions and rearrange their dispositions; you disenfranchise their exclusions and their exceptionalisms.[4] Occupation rearranges the extant divisions that are, in their nature, exclusionary by coordinating a new ensemble of parts that no longer function as they had, whose structure of interest no longer holds. Other interests and divisions might (and likely will) emerge. The nature of play and repetition is such that new games, and thus new ways of participating in the game, emerge. But their individuation is not determined. This is the aesthetic point to Rancière's politics: when a new configuration of forces emerges out of an improper occupancy the governing structures of interest divert and dissemble. Hence the power of the demos, the popular, *les communs*, which is more than etymologically related to an immanent power of division. (Recall the Indo-European "da" that links democracy with division.)

If this description evokes a certain sense of aesthetic modernism, that should not surprise us. To the extent that Rancière is a peculiar kind of formalist (the kind that believes in forms imminent to a scene rather than as transcendental), he is also a peculiar kind of modernist, and I admit that one of the structuring ambitions of this book is to track the uniqueness of his demotic modernism. In this respect it is difficult to imagine books like *Disagreement* or *Aisthesis* as offering anything other than a counterhistory of modernism that substitutes the centrality of the modernist spectator/ critic who must judge the value of the work with the autodidactic practitioner of an art that has no name, of a gesture that has no home in the Pantheon of deeds, of a thought that has no discernible context.[5] Hence his affinity for the classic modernist trope of innervation and his reconfiguration of it as dissensus. Stimulating the nerves of the common people is a grave danger, Rancière explains: "Lamentation about a surfeit of consumable commodities and images was first and foremost a depiction of democratic society as one in which there are too many individuals capable of appropriating words, images and forms of lived experience. Such was in fact the great anxiety of nineteenth century elites: anxiety about the circulation of these unprecedented forms of lived experience, likely to give any passerby, visitor or reader materials liable to contribute to the reconfiguration of her life-world."[6] In these now too familiar reversals of critical common sense, Rancière displays the dynamics of inequality by inverting our intuitions about aesthetic and political criticism, as he also does in his refusals to identify what art is and in his resistance to formulate terms of political judgment.[7] It's almost as if his radically democratic countermodernism wants to answer the call of Marx's eleventh thesis by showing that there always have been scenes of change and not just objects of philosophical interpretation. For wherever there is an object of interpretation there is also an emergent sensorial world, a partition of the sensible, that transforms the conditions of political and aesthetic living, a scene of radical mediation.

This is one way we might understand that Rancière doesn't give us a program for overcoming inequalities or a hermeneutic theory of meaning. Such a programmatic sense of *theory* would require the application of virtues and objectives that are external to the doing and knowing of those occupying the lines of division that constitute the particularity of the scene. The implementation of equality through a science of emancipation requires the transmission of and submission to ways of doing and knowing that are not immanent to the situation, and thus do not belong to the participants in play. In its stead Rancière provides us with instances, examples, and practices of occupation immanent to specific micro situations. Such affective pragmatics involve popular ways of doing, like the ornamental arrangements of Agee and Evans's sharecroppers or the appropriations of scenes of enunciation by those who do not have the capacity "to guarantee the reference of what [they say]."[8] These scenes populate Rancière's writings; they are legion, almost as if his ambition was less to provide his reader with illustrative examples that could be interpreted, explained, or reproduced than to generate in and through his orthographic gestures "the roar of an urban theatrocracy."[9] His sentiments generate a mode of reading and writing that enacts the simultaneity of the aesthetic and the political; but more than this, they belie a practice of reading and writing that puts the *ignorant gestu* on display as a power and force of occupation distensive across his pages.

This, I note, is a central though often underappreciated feature of his thought that is available once we shift our readerly mode from the analytic unpacking of a Porphyrian morphology to a sentimental disposition that looks to Rancière's styles of writing and ways of arranging words—and scenes—on a page. For what emerges from the mode of reading I have proposed throughout is a disposition toward the distensive amorphousness in any organization of sentences, words, images, examples, concepts, ideas, vistas, auralities, and polemics that gives visibility to the power of occupancy as transformative to any given arrangement. Thus when I say that the shock of appearance populates Rancière's writings, what I mean is that he writes as if to occupy his works with disjunctive moments of dissensus that jar our ability to process scholarly interest. And this, in and of itself, is an aesthetics and politics for reading and writing theory. For him, political action is not determined by any specific skill in organizing interests or verifying truths; politics is aesthetic for Rancière because it involves the deployment of popular practices for occupying times and spaces and their alterations. Hence his persistent invocations of the makings and doings and happenings of everyday persons and his accounting for these as autodidactic, impersonal partakings that anyone and everyone can occupy because they belong to no one. Herein lies the full force of Rancière's aesthetics and politics: the incipience of an affective pragmatics for the occupation of everyday life.

NOTES

Preface

1. Jacques Rancière, *The Method of Equality: Interviews with Laurent Jeanpierre and Dork Zabunyan* (Hoboken, NJ: John Wiley and Sons, 2016), 65.

2. Rancière, *The Method of Equality*, 66.

3. Ronald Beiner, *Political Judgment* (London: Methuen, 1983); Hannah Arendt and Ronald Beiner, *Lectures on Kant's Political Philosophy* (Chicago: University of Chicago Press, 1989); Kennan Ferguson, *The Politics of Judgment: Aesthetics, Identity, and Political Theory* (Lanham, MD: Lexington Books, 2007); Hina Nazar, *Enlightened Sentiments: Judgment and Autonomy in the Age of Sensibility* (New York: Fordham University Press, 2012); Sheldon S. Wolin, *Politics and Vision: Continuity and Innovation in Western Political Thought* (Princeton, NJ: Princeton University Press, 2009).

4. "Incommensurable," *OED Online*, accessed October 11, 2016, http://www.oed.com/view/Entry/93659#eid803570.

5. Rancière, *The Method of Equality*, 67.

6. The most famous instance of such denunciations is expressed in the emergence of New French Thought. See especially Luc Ferry and Alain Renaut, *French Philosophy of the Sixties: An Essay on Antihumanism* (Amherst: University of Massachusetts Press, 1990). For Rancière's contributions to questions of political failure(s), see Jacques Rancière, *Staging the People: The Proletarian and His Double* (London: Verso, 2011) and *The Intellectual and His People: Staging the People*, vol. 2 (London: Verso, 2012).

7. Bonnie Honig adopts this position in her discussion of the "*taking* foreigner" that refers to practices of "enacting the redistribution of those powers, rights, and privileges that define a community and order it hierarchically." Bonnie Honig, *Democracy and the Foreigner* (Princeton, NJ: Princeton University Press, 2009), 8. It is possible to read *Democracy and the Foreigner* as at once an extension of and engagement with Rancière's account of democratic participation.

8. Linda M. G. Zerilli, *Feminism and the Abyss of Freedom* (Chicago: University of Chicago Press, 2005), 141. In her most recent book, *A Democratic Theory of Judgment* (Chicago: University of Chicago Press, 2016), Zerilli develops a rich philosophical account of democratic critical judgment and its world-building possibilities. But though she deftly defends the position of a post-Kantian mode of Arendtian reflective judgment that is absent the demand of conceptual application, she nonetheless holds to the application of the concept of judgment for democratic life.

9. On this point Zerilli is close to Wolin's admonition against the theory application model, whereby "theories are likened to appliances which are 'plugged into' political life." Sheldon S. Wolin, "Political Theory as a Vocation," *American Political Science Review* 63, no. 4 (1969): 1062–82, doi:10.1017/S000305540026320X.

10. Arendt and Beiner, *Lectures on Kant's Political Philosophy.*

11. Rancière, *The Method of Equality*, 67.

12. In this Rancière is in company with James Tully's articulation of practices of what he calls "diverse citizenship" and his distinction between a critical theory and a critical ethos. See James Tully, *Public Philosophy in a New Key*, vol. 1: *Democracy and Civic Freedom* (Cambridge: Cambridge University Press, 2008), esp. chapter 3, and *On Global Citizenship: James Tully in Dialogue* (London: Bloomsbury Academic, 2014), esp. 33–73.

13. Some may wish to constellate such a sensibility with modernism, as I do in my concluding remarks.

Introduction

1. Oliver Davis, *Jacques Rancière* (Hoboken, NJ: John Wiley, 2013); Oliver Davis, *Rancière Now* (Cambridge, UK: Polity, 2013); Samuel A. Chambers, *The Lessons of Rancière* (New York: Oxford University Press, 2014); Joseph J. Tanke, *Jacques Rancière: An Introduction* (New York: A&C Black, 2011); Todd May, *The Political Thought of Jacques Rancière: Creating Equality* (Edinburgh: Edinburgh University Press, 2008) ; Todd May, *Contemporary Political Movements and the Thought of Jacques Rancière: Equality in Action* (Edinburgh: Edinburgh University Press, 2010); Gabriel Rockhill and Philip Watts, *Jacques Rancière: History, Politics, Aesthetics* (Durham, NC: Duke University Press, 2009); Jean-Philippe Deranty, *Jacques Rancière: Key Concepts* (New York: Routledge, 2014); Charles Bingham and Gert Biesta, *Jacques Rancière: Education, Truth, Emancipation* (New York: A&C Black, 2010).

2. Oliver Davis and Jacques Rancière, "On Aisthesis: An Interview," in Davis, *Rancière Now*, 202. Also see Peter Hallward, "Staging Equality," *New Left Review* 2, no. 37 (2006): 109–29.

3. I adapt the term *affective pragmatics* from Brian Massumi's discussion of micropolitics in *Politics of Affect* (Hoboken, NJ: John Wiley, 2015), 41.

4. Jacques Rancière, *Proletarian Nights: The Workers' Dream in Nineteenth-Century France* (London: Verso, 2014), ix.

5. Tobias Menely, *The Animal Claim: Sensibility and the Creaturely Voice* (Chicago: University of Chicago Press, 2015); Anthony Pagden, *The Enlightenment: And Why It Still Matters* (New York: Random House, 2013); James Chandler, *An Archaeology of Sympathy: The Sentimental Mode in Literature and Cinema* (Chicago: University of Chicago Press, 2013).

6. On recent debates in formalist aesthetics, see Caroline Levine, *Forms: Whole, Rhythm, Hierarchy, Network* (Princeton, NJ: Princeton University Press, 2015); Sandra Macpherson, "A Little Formalism," ELH 82, no. 2 (2015): 385–405; Frances Ferguson, "Jane Austen, *Emma*, and the Impact of Form," MLQ: *Modern Language Quarterly* 61, no. 1 (2000): 157–80.

7. Rancière, *The Method of Equality*, 67.

8. Hallward, "Staging Equality," esp. 126–29.

9. Aletta J. Norval, "'Writing a Name in the Sky': Rancière, Cavell, and the Possibility of Egalitarian Inscription," *American Political Science Review* 106, no. 4 (2012): 823.

10. Such an orientation to theoretical work finds inspiration from the works of Elisabeth Robin Anker, *Orgies of Feeling: Melodrama and the Politics of Freedom* (Durham, NC: Duke University Press, 2014); Chandler, *An Archaeology of Sympathy*; Anita Chari, *A Political Economy of the Senses: Neoliberalism, Reification, Critique* (New York: Columbia University Press, 2015); Amanda Anderson, *The Way We Argue Now: A Study in the Cultures of Theory* (Princeton, NJ: Princeton University Press, 2005); and especially Theo Davis, *Ornamental Aesthetics: The Poetry of Attending in Thoreau, Dickinson, and Whitman* (Oxford: Oxford University Press, 2016).

11. Chandler, *An Archaeology of Sympathy*, xiv.

12. As I noted in the preface, Rancière here is proximate to the account of "diverse citizenship" in James Tully, *On Global Citizenship: James Tully in Dialogue* (London: Bloomsbury Academic, 2014) and *Public Philosophy in a New Key*, vol. 1: *Democracy and Civic Freedom* (Cambridge: Cambridge University Press, 2008). Also noteworthy is Tully's distinction between a critical theory and a critical ethos. My own deployment of the language of sentiments that invokes "dispositions," "sensibilities," "moods," and the like is intended to expand on Tully's distinction in the hope of taking the insights further away from an identification (for good and bad) with ethical theories. Hence my privileging of the term *critical dispositions* rather than Tully's "critical ethos." On the characterological dimensions of theoretical inquiry, also see part 3: "Ethos and Argument" in Amanda Anderson's *The Way We Argue Now*.

13. Jacques Rancière, Rachel Bowlby, and Davide Panagia, "Ten Theses on Politics," *Theory and Event* 5, no. 3 (2001).

14. Richard Grusin, "Radical Mediation," *Critical Inquiry* 42, no. 1 (2015): 124–48.

15. Jacques Rancière, *The Ignorant Schoolmaster: Five Lessons in Intellectual Emancipation* (Stanford: Stanford University Press, 1991).

16. Jacques Rancière, *The Future of the Image*, trans. Gregory Elliott, reprint ed. (London: Verso, 2009), 42.

17. On the status of the commons in Rancière's thought, see Kristin Ross, *Communal Luxury: The Political Imaginary of the Paris Commune* (London: Verso, 2015), and Bruno Bosteels, "The Mexican Commune," in *Communism in the 21st Century*, ed. Shannon Brincat (Santa Barbara, CA: Greenwood, 2014). See also Thierry Briault and Jacques Rancière, "Entretien avec Jacques Rancière sur la Plastique et le Sens Commun," *Club de Mediapart*, November 25, 2015, https://blogs.mediapart.fr/thierry-briault/blog/251115 /entretien-avec-jacques-Rancière-sur-la-plastique-et-le-sens-commun. Here Rancière says this:

> Si "partage du sensible" peut se traduire par "sens commun," c'est à condition de bien préciser le sens de la notion. "Sens commun" chez moi ne désigne jamais une faculté de juger ou une disposition à la communauté qui appartiendrait à tous. Rien à voir donc avec un principe de charité ou d'intercompréhension. . . . Sens commun pour moi désigne l'ensemble des relations qui déterminent un monde sensible commun en déterminant, en même temps que ce qui apparaît, la façon dont nous pouvons le nommer et le penser. Cela désigne les conditions de notre expérience, c'est-à-dire à la fois la texture de ce que nous éprouvons et la capacité que nous avons de l'éprouver selon la place que nous occupons dans ce monde commun. Non pas une capacité partagée par tous mais le réseau de relations entre l'être, le perceptible, le dicible, le pensable et le faisable qui détermine les capacités des uns et des autres. . . . Il est une structure qui, à la fois, nous donne en partage un monde commun "sensé" et détermine notre capacité ou incapacité à produire du sens et à participer au commun. Le sens commun, en ce sens, est toujours *un* sens commun déterminé. Ce qui veut dire aussi qu'il n'est pas "la" structure à laquelle tout sujet est assujetti, qu'il est transformable et transformé par les actes qui tissent d'autres sens communs dans les interstices du partage dominant du sensible et éventuellement contre lui. Il est constamment tissé et retissé par les actes qui mettent des corps en rapport les uns aux autres dans des espaces et des temps et selon des protocoles de parole particuliers. Il est tissé et retissé par le choix de mettre ensemble des mots, des formes, des images, des gestes, des mouvements, des sons, des temps, des espaces.

> [If partition of the sensible is potentially translatable as "common sense" it may be so if we specify a precise sense of the notion. "Common sense" for me does not refer to a faculty of judgment or a disposition that belongs to the entirety of a community. It

has nothing to do, in other words, with a notion of sympathy or inter-comprehension. . . . Common sense for me designates an ensemble of relations that coordinate a sensible world in common by establishing, at the same time as what appears, the manner in which what appears may be named and thought. This designates the conditions of our experience, which is to say at the same time the fabric of sensations and our capacities to sense according to where we are in relation to a common. Common sense is not a capacity shared by all but a network of relations between being, the perceptible, the sayable, the thinkable, the do-able that determines the capacities of everyone and everything in this weave of relations. It is a structure that at once provides a sharing of a sensible world in common and determines our capacities or incapacities of generating a sense and participation of an in-common. A common sense, in this sense, is always a particular determined sense. Which also means that there is not a single structure of subjectification for subjects, that any structure is alterable and transformed by acts that weave other senses in common within the interstices of a dominant partition of the sensible and, eventually, in contest with the dominant mode of partitioning. A common sense is consistently woven and rewoven by capacities that place bodies in relation to each other within spatiotemporal coordinates, and according to protocols of specific words. It is woven and rewoven by the willingness to assemble words, forms, images, gestures, movements, sounds, temporalities, and spatialities. (My translation)]

18. See Jonathan Sterne's discussion of perceptual technics in his *MP3: The Meaning of a Format* (Durham, NC: Duke University Press, 2012).

19. Frances Ferguson, "Our I. A. Richards Moment: The Machine and Its Adjustments," in *Theory Aside*, ed. Jason Potts and Daniel Stout (Durham, NC: Duke University Press Books, 2014), 262.

20. Davide Panagia, *The Political Life of Sensation* (Durham, NC: Duke University Press, 2010).

21. Rancière, *The Ignorant Schoolmaster.*

22. Ross, *Communal Luxury*, 46–47.

23. Rancière here is close to William Connolly and Connolly's treatment of the desire to punish. "The desire to punish," Connolly affirms, "crystallizes at that point where the shocking, vicious character of a case blocks inquiry into its conditions, repressing examination of uncertainties and ambiguities pervading the very concepts through which it is judged. Where astonishment terminates inquiry, the element of revenge is consolidated." William E. Connolly, *The Ethos of Pluralization* (Minneapolis: University of Minnesota Press, 1995), 47. Though Connolly is not writing about Rancière, or about judgment per se, it is notable that there is a shared sensibility here regarding the disavowal of a sensation of shock vis-à-vis an experience, and how that dissensual experience, when felt within a judgment scenario, closes off the very possibility of inquiry. In parallel ways

both Rancière and Connolly wish to move away from a system of judgment that denies the productive political work of dissensus.

24. Jacques Rancière, *The Names of History: On the Poetics of Knowledge* (Minneapolis: University of Minnesota Press, 1994); Rancière, *The Future of the Image*, 41.

25. Rancière, *The Names of History*.

26. Pagden, *The Enlightenment*, 55.

27. Ross, *Communal Luxury*, 53.

28. Adrian Rifkin, "Cultural Movement and the Paris Commune," *Art History* 2, no. 2 (1979): 201–20.

29. Ross, *Communal Luxury*, 52.

30. Panagia, *The Political Life of Sensation*, 21–44.

31. Jacques Lévy, Juliette Rennes, and David Zerbib, "Jacques Rancière: 'Les territoires de la pensée partagée,'" *Revue électronique des sciences humaines et sociales*, January 8, 2007, http://www.espacestemps.net/articles/jacques-Rancière-les-territoires-de-la-pensee -partagee/.

32. Jacques Rancière, *Althusser's Lesson* (London: Bloomsbury, 2011); Jacques Rancière, *The Emancipated Spectator* (London: Verso, 2014).

33. Charles Taylor, "Interpretations and the Sciences of Man," in *Philosophical Papers*, vol. 2: *Philosophy and the Human Sciences* (Cambridge: Cambridge University Press, 1985), 15–57; Quentin Skinner, "Meaning and Understanding in the History of Ideas," in *Meaning and Context: Quentin Skinner and His Critics*, ed. James Tully (Cambridge, UK: Polity, 1988), 29–67.

34. *Style indirect libre*, or "free indirect discourse" (as it is often translated in English), is a style of prose writing associated with the rise of the novel and especially associated with the works of Austen and Flaubert. It is characterized by the ability of the novel's narrator to give voice to the thoughts, feelings, ideas, and sensations of characters without the need or benefit of attributional prefaces like "he surmised" or "she thought to herself." Its effects are many, but most notable is free indirect style's ability to create an intimacy with the characters, as if we are privy to their mental states without having to be forewarned about them. But also important is its ability to render the authority of words indistinct so that the status of the authorial voice is displaced, making it difficult, if not at times impossible, to distinguish among author, narrator, and character. This latter point is of central importance to the tradition of French political theory from which Rancière draws. Though it is beyond the scope of this book, the availability and repeated engagement with Flaubert in twentieth-century French philosophy helps explain the strain of French literary and political thinking that challenges the authority of the author, as in

Roland Barthes's "The Death of the Author" in *Image-Music-Text* (New York: Macmillan, 1978) and Michel Foucault's "What Is an Author?" in *The Foucault Reader* (New York: Pantheon, 1984). Free indirect style thus allows for the possibility of displacing authorial intention in speech and language. For an excellent discussion of this, see especially Frances Ferguson's essay "Now It's Personal: D. A. Miller and Too-Close Reading," *Critical Inquiry* 41, no. 3 (2015): 521–40.

35. Martha C. Nussbaum, *Love's Knowledge: Essays on Philosophy and Literature* (New York: Oxford University Press, 1992), 7. Another way of stating the distinction between Nussbaum's sense of the literature's purposiveness and Rancière's sense of the aesthetic's unpurposiveness is that Rancière does not sign on to Nussbaum's Aristotelian hylomorphism that imagines an appropriate relation between form and content, as Nussbaum explains: "There may then be certain plausible views about the nature of the relevant portions of human life that cannot be housed within that form without generating a peculiar implicit contradiction" (7). For Nussbaum's project, content and form are bound in necessary ways, but it is precisely that relation of necessity that Rancière's scenographies undo to engender "a peculiar implicit contradiction."

36. Jacques Rancière, *Aisthesis: Scenes from the Aesthetic Regime of Art*, trans. Zakir Paul (London: Verso, 2013), xi.

37. Rancière, *Aisthesis*, 2.

38. Rancière, *Aisthesis*, 3–4.

39. Rancière, *Aisthesis*, 6.

40. On disinterest in Rancière see Panagia, *The Political Life of Sensation*, 21–45.

41. Jane Bennett, *Vibrant Matter: A Political Ecology of Things* (Durham, NC: Duke University Press, 2009), 3.

42. Martin Heidegger, *Being and Time* (New York: HarperCollins, 2008); Sharon R. Krause, *Freedom beyond Sovereignty: Reconstructing Liberal Individualism* (Chicago: University of Chicago Press, 2015). With this provocation I am not suggesting an indebtedness on the part of Rancière either to a Heideggerian discussion of conspicuousness and worlding nor to a substantially modified account of liberal individualism (Krause). What I am suggesting is that there is an elective affinity of sensibilities in this assembly of authors and ideas that is at once compelling and productive for our appreciation of Rancière's scenographic assemblages.

43. Jonathan Havercroft and David Owen, "Soul-Blindness, Police Orders and Black Lives Matter: Wittgenstein, Cavell, and Rancière," *Political Theory*, July 11, 2016, 11.

44. Davide Panagia, *Ten Theses for an Aesthetics of Politics*, Forerunners: Ideas First (Minneapolis: University of Minnesota Press, 2016).

45. Ludwig Wittgenstein, *Philosophical Investigations*, 3rd ed. (New York: Pearson, 1973), section 524, p. 142e.

46. Rancière, *Aisthesis*, 11.

47. Grusin, "Radical Mediation," 124–48.

Chapter 1. Rancière's Partager

1. Jean-Jacques Rousseau, *Rousseau: "The Discourses" and Other Early Political Writings*, ed. Victor Gourevitch (Cambridge: Cambridge University Press, 1997), 161.

2. Jacques Rancière, *The Philosopher and His Poor*, ed. Andrew Parker, trans. Corinne Oster and John Drury (Durham, NC: Duke University Press, 2004), 225.

3. The contemporary writer who has done the most work on radical mediation and method in contemporary political thought is Michael Shapiro. See especially *Studies in Trans-Disciplinary Method: After the Aesthetic Turn* (New York: Routledge, 2013).

4. *Partager* has been translated as "division," "distribution," and "partition," as in the division, distribution, or partition of the sensible. Though all of these translations are accurate, none of them accurately attends to the distensive nature of the aesthetico-political operation of radical mediation that *partager* does. Thus, to avoid constant specifications of its distensions I retain the French throughout.

5. J. David Bolter and Richard A. Grusin, *Remediation: Understanding New Media* (Cambridge, MA: MIT Press, 2000).

6. Richard Grusin, "Radical Mediation," *Critical Inquiry* 42, no. 1 (2015): 124–48.

7. Grusin, "Radical Mediation," 129.

8. Jacques Rancière, "Politics, Identification, and Subjectivization," *October* 61 (1992): 61.

9. Rancière, "Politics, Identification, and Subjectivization," 61.

10. Jürgen Habermas, *The Philosophical Discourse of Modernity: Twelve Lectures*, trans. Frederick G. Lawrence, reprint ed. (Cambridge, MA: MIT Press, 1990); Pierre Bourdieu, *Distinction: A Social Critique of the Judgement of Taste* (Cambridge, MA: Harvard University Press, 1984); Martin Jay, "'The Aesthetic Ideology' as Ideology; or, What Does It Mean to Aestheticize Politics?," *Cultural Critique*, no. 21 (1992): 41–61; Terry Eagleton, *The Ideology of the Aesthetic* (Hoboken, NJ: Wiley, 1991).

11. Murray Krieger, *Ekphrasis: The Illusion of the Natural Sign* (Baltimore: Johns Hopkins University Press, 1992).

12. Rancière, "Politics, Identification, and Subjectivization," 61. Crucial here is Rancière's

repurposing of the term *proletarian* from the Latin *proletarii*, meaning "prolific people." The Latin *proles* forms the root of both *prolific* and *proletarian*. In ancient Roman society proletarians were those who merely lived to reproduce progeny, whose only purpose was reproduction. In this sense they were outcasts because excessive and supernumerary. Emphasizing the classification of prolific and multiple, Rancière repurposes the term *proletarian* to point to any excessive element of in-betweenness that undoes extant orders of classification. The proletarian is thus not a specific subject position; it is a formal category that for Rancière refers to an excess of doing that is out of turn and outside the order of time. In short, *proletarian* regards the interstitial power of the supernumerary multiple.

13. Michael Freeden, *Ideologies and Political Theory: A Conceptual Approach* (Oxford: Clarendon, 1998), 75–91.

14. Freeden, *Ideologies and Political Theory*.

15. Jacques Rancière, *La Leçon d'Althusser* (Paris: Gallimard, 1975), and *Althusser's Lesson* (London: Bloomsbury, 2011). For consistency's sake, and unless otherwise noted, I will be citing from the English translation.

16. Samuel A. Chambers, *The Lessons of Rancière* (Oxford: Oxford University Press, 2014), 123–56; Emmanuel Renault, "The Many Marx of Jacques Rancière," in *Jacques Rancière and the Contemporary Scene: The Philosophy of Radical Equality*, ed. Jean-Philippe Deranty and Alison Ross (New York: A&C Black, 2012).

17. Rancière, *Althusser's Lesson*, xiv.

18. Louis Althusser, *For Marx*, trans. Ben Brewster (London: Verso, 2006), 32. See Thomas S. Kuhn, *The Structure of Scientific Revolutions: 50th Anniversary Edition* (Chicago: University of Chicago Press, 2012).

19. Louis Althusser, *Lenin and Philosophy, and Other Essays* (New York: Monthly Review Press, 1971). Please note that the following comments on Althusser's theory of mediation are based on my reading of his "Ideology and Ideological State Apparatuses" essay, esp. 148–86.

20. As I explain below, the apparatus metaphor as a technical device for signal transmission is significant to Althusser's cybernetic account of power in ideology.

21. Fredric Jameson, *The Political Unconscious: Narrative as a Socially Symbolic Act* (Ithaca, NY: Cornell University Press, 1991), 39.

22. On false homologies, see Jameson, *The Political Unconscious*, 41.

23. Jameson, *The Political Unconscious*, 41.

24. Jameson, *The Political Unconscious*, 41.

25. Rancière, *Althusser's Lesson*, xiv.

26. Michael Suk-Young Chwe, *Rational Ritual: Culture, Coordination, and Common Knowledge* (Princeton, NJ: Princeton University Press, 2003).

27. Rancière, *Althusser's Lesson*, xx; Kristin Ross, *May '68 and Its Afterlives* (Chicago: University of Chicago Press, 2004), 86.

28. In subsequent work Rancière will articulate this dynamic as the representational regime of art, or mimesis, which effects a "concordance between the arts founded on a new coincidence between the space of language and the space of things." Jacques Rancière, *Mute Speech: Literature, Critical Theory, and Politics* (New York: Columbia University Press, 2011), 137.

29. Alain Brossat, "La notion de dispositif chez Michel Foucault," in *Miroir, appareils et autres dispositifs*, ed. Soko Phay-Vakalis (Paris: Editions l'Harmattan, 2009), 201.

30. James Chandler, *An Archaeology of Sympathy: The Sentimental Mode in Literature and Cinema* (Chicago: University of Chicago Press, 2013), xiv.

31. Rancière, *Althusser's Lesson*, xv–xvi.

32. Jacques Rancière, *Aisthesis: Scenes from the Aesthetic Regime of Art*, trans. Zakir Paul (London: Verso, 2013), xi.

33. Victor Tausk, "On the Origin of the 'Influence Machine' in Schizophrenia," *Journal of Psychotherapy Practice and Research* 1, no. 2 (1992): 185–206.

34. Melvin Rogers's recent critique of contemporary accounts of republicanism raises a similar problem: namely how can such theoretical positions vis-à-vis the problem of domination be viable when the writers participating in resuscitating the republican critique of domination ignore the historical fact of racial domination in the United States and equally ignore an entire series of writings by early African American political thinkers who may have something to say about domination, this despite the fact that their way of writing, and their mode of saying, is not homologous with a discourse of republican theory as it is perceived, read, and accepted in contemporary theoretical circles. See Melvin Rogers, "Race and Republicanism: Early African American Political Thought," *La Revue internationale de philosophie*, forthcoming.

35. Jacques Rancière, Fulvia Carnevale, and John Kelsey, "Art of the Possible: Fulvia Carnevale and John Kelsey in Conversation with Jacques Rancière," *Artforum* 45, no. 7 (2007): 257.

36. The language of transfiguration here is indebted to Arthur Coleman Danto, *The Transfiguration of the Commonplace: A Philosophy of Art* (Cambridge, MA: Harvard University Press, 1981). The language of social isomorphism is from Jacob T. Levy, *Rational-*

ism, Pluralism, and Freedom (New York: Oxford University Press, 2015). There is a strong family resemblance between Rancière's discussion of the *partager* of the part who have no-part and Levy's treatment of intermediate groups in his discussion of pluralism and isomorphism. Indeed, Levy's suspicion of what he refers to as "the fallacy of composition" (75) and his critique of congruence (53–55) offer compellingly proximate insights to Rancière's critique of consensus theories of deliberative democracy as well as his critique of Aristotelian poetics. In part this is no doubt due to the fact that both Levy and Rancière are sentimental theorists, as I've defined them. Hence Levy's ambition and call to "resist easy narratives of harmony" (8).

37. Jacques Rancière, *The Politics of Aesthetics* (New York: Continuum, 2004), 12.

38. Davide Panagia and Jacques Rancière, "Dissenting Words: A Conversation with Jacques Rancière," *Diacritics* 30, no. 2 (2000): 115.

39. Rancière, *The Politics of Aesthetics*, 39–40.

40. Jacques Rancière, *Disagreement: Politics and Philosophy* (Minneapolis: University of Minnesota Press, 2004), 39.

41. Rancière, *Disagreement*, 39.

42. Rancière, *The Politics of Aesthetics*.

43. Rancière, *The Politics of Aesthetics*, 23. See also Panagia and Rancière, "Dissenting Words," 116.

44. Bonnie Honig relies on this dynamic for her reading of Antigone's conspiracy "with language to work the interval between lamentation and *logos*, singularity and equality, between the infinite *aiai* of tragedy and the finite *aei* of the city." Bonnie Honig, *Antigone, Interrupted* (Cambridge: Cambridge University Press, 2013), 146. Crucial to this reading is Honig's development of the concept of conspiracy, also developed in James Martel's reading of Walter Benjamin, which describes a transformational practice of mediation *in* the in-between. "Benjamin's conspiracy," Martel explains, "involves a different form of relationality than our understanding of politics usually involves. The word 'conspiracy' (in English) comes from the Latin meaning 'those who breathe together,' implying a closeness and interrelationality in one moment and one place. The German term *verschwörern* similarly suggests a relationality, literally: those who swear together." James Martel, *Textual Conspiracies: Walter Benjamin, Idolatry, and Political Theory* (Ann Arbor: University of Michigan Press, 2011), 17. The idea of a swearing conspiracy as the taking of a word out of turn and out of place together is something shared by Honig's Antigone, Martel's Benjamin, and Rancière's no-part.

45. Rancière, *The Politics of Aesthetics*, 13.

46. Panagia and Rancière, "Dissenting Words," 125.

47. Even in Colin Koopman's generously expansive account of the Kantian critical tradition, it is difficult to see Rancière fitting comfortably therein—this despite Rancière's intellectual debt to Foucault's work. Colin Koopman, *Genealogy as Critique: Foucault and the Problems of Modernity* (Bloomington: Indiana University Press, 2013).

48. John Guillory, "How Scholars Read," ADE *Bulletin*, no. 146 (Fall 2008): 12. It should be noted that Guillory is careful in adumbrating a variety of forms of intensive reading practices.

49. Lima, *Visual Complexity*, 25.

50. Lima, *Visual Complexity*, 27–28.

51. I elaborate this further in Davide Panagia, "A Theory of Aspects: Media Participation and Political Theory," *New Literary History* 45, no. 4 (2014): 527–48 and *Ten Theses for an Aesthetics of Politics*, Forerunners: Ideas First (Minneapolis: University of Minnesota Press, 2016), esp. Thesis 1: "On Advenience."

52. Here I am indebted to Liam Young's media archaeology of the list, its material form, and its network function. See Liam Young, "On Lists and Networks: An Archaeology of Form," *Amodern 2: Archaeology*, 2013, http://amodern.net/article/on-lists-and-networks/.

53. Rancière, *The Politics of Aesthetics*, 15.

54. Rancière, *The Politics of Aesthetics*, 15.

55. Freeden, *Ideologies and Political Theory*, 68–75.

56. Martel, *Textual Conspiracies*.

57. Rancière, *The Politics of Aesthetics*, 14.

58. Rancière, *The Politics of Aesthetics*, 14.

Chapter 2. Rancière's Police Poetics

1. For an excellent account of that work within the context of Rancière's oeuvre, see Jason Frank, "Logical Revolts: Jacques Rancière and Political Subjectivization," *Political Theory* 43, no. 2 (2015): 249–61.

2. Jacques Rancière, *The Politics of Aesthetics* (New York: Continuum, 2004), 36.

3. Lewis and Short's *A Latin Dictionary* entry for *decorus* lists "becoming," "fitting," "seemly," "proper," "suitable," "decorous," "shining," and "a beautiful thing" as possible translations for the term. Charlton T. Lewis and Charles Short, eds., "Dĕcōrus," in *A Latin*

Dictionary, accessed April 15, 2016, http://www.perseus.tufts.edu/hopper/text?doc =Perseus%3Atext%3A1999.04.0059%3Aentry%3Ddecorus.

4. Nancy S. Struever, *The Language of History in the Renaissance: Rhetoric and Historical Consciousness in Florentine Humanism* (Princeton, NJ: Princeton University Press, 2015), 67, 68.

5. Robert Hariman, *Political Style: The Artistry of Power* (Chicago: University of Chicago Press, 2010), 19.

6. Rancière states, "I call this regime *poetic* in the sense that it identifies the arts—what the Classical Age would later call the 'fine arts'—within a classification of ways of doing and making, and it consequently defines proper ways of doing and making as well as means of assessing imitations. I call it *representative* insofar as it is the notion of representation or *mimesis* that organizes these ways of doing, making, seeing, and judging" (*The Politics of Aesthetics*, 17).

7. Jacques Rancière, *Mute Speech: Literature, Critical Theory, and Politics* (New York: Columbia University Press, 2011), 97.

8. Jacob T. Levy, *Rationalism, Pluralism, and Freedom* (New York: Oxford University Press, 2015).

9. This said, the account I will give is closely aligned with the interpretation of *Poetics* offered by Stephen Halliwell, especially in chapter 5 of *Aristotle's Poetics* (Chicago: University of Chicago Press, 1986), 138–67.

10. Aristotle, *Poetics*, in *The Basic Works of Aristotle* (New York: Random House, 2009), 1448a2.

11. Aristotle, *Poetics*, 1448b5.

12. Aristotle, *Poetics*, 1451a31–35. Rancière's aesthetic and political commitment will be precisely to dislocate the interconnections of this whole.

13. Aristotle, *Poetics*, 1451b33–35.

14. Aristotle, *Poetics*, 1454a33–39.

15. Aristotle, *Poetics*, 1460b9.

16. Another way of saying this is that what Aristotle puts on the table is a politics of representation, an account of politics that is dependent on a theory of representation (i.e., mimesis), and what Rancière wants to show is how an aesthetics of representation is a limit on democracy. The possibility of "democracy after representation is something that Simon Tormey examines in *The End of Representative Politics* (New York: John Wiley & Sons, 2015), esp. 125–49.

17. Aristotle, *Poetics*, 1457b7–10.

18. Paul Ricoeur, *The Rule of Metaphor: Multi-Disciplinary Studies of the Creation of Meaning in Language* (Toronto: University of Toronto Press, 1981), 18. Also see Jacques Derrida, "White Mythology," in *Margins of Philosophy* (Chicago: University of Chicago Press, 1982). Derrida's study of metaphor is a reflection on the forgetfulness of language of its own origins, hence his Nietzschean reading of metaphor as a site of *usure*—of both use and erasure, of wornness and forgetting and thus a kind of taking for granted of the naturalization of meanings. That said, central to Derrida's reading is the assumption that the discussion of metaphor in the history of philosophy is of a part with the Western tradition of metaphysics to the extent that that history is one of identity and difference and their relation.

19. Aristotle, *Poetics*, 1459a5–8.

20. Aristotle, *Poetics*, 1450b34–36.

21. Aristotle, *Poetics*, 1450a35.

22. As a brief aside, I can think of no better definition of Rancière's police than an isomorphic system of "metaphysical emplotment."

23. Aristotle, *Metaphysics*, in *The Basic Works of Aristotle* (New York: Random House, 2009), 1032a11 (book 7, ch. 7).

24. Aristotle, *Metaphysics*, 1032b23.

25. Aristotle, *Metaphysics*, 1030a10.

26. Aristotle, *Metaphysics*, 1073b1.

27. Jacques Rancière, *The Future of the Image*, trans. Gregory Elliott, reprint ed. (London: Verso, 2009), 104: "Mimesis was the principle not of resemblance but of a certain codification and distribution of resemblances."

28. Paul Ricoeur, *Time and Narrative*, vol. 1, trans. Kathleen McLaughlin and David Pellauer (Chicago: University of Chicago Press, 1990).

29. This is a point that Ricoeur also raises in his studies on metaphor, especially the distinction he makes between an interactive and a substitutional view of metaphor. See "Metaphor and the Problem of Hermeneutics," in Paul Ricoeur and John B. Thompson, *Hermeneutics and the Human Sciences: Essays on Language, Action and Interpretation* (Cambridge: Cambridge University Press, 1981), 165–81.

30. Ricoeur, "Metaphor and the Problem of Hermeneutics," 36.

31. This is exactly the inverse operation that Ricoeur finds in Aristotle's *Nicomachean Ethics*, where, he notes (citing *Poetics*, 1105a30 ff.), character precedes action in the order of ethical qualities.

32. Ricoeur, *Time and Narrative*, 38, 40.

33. In part 4 of the *Poetics*, Aristotle introduces one final element to his general theory of muthos: rhythm. Here he describes how tragedy acquires "a tone of dignity" (1449a21) with the conventional use of iambic meters, which are the most speakable of meters (1449a25), and he returns to this observation in his discussion of diction in part 20. One learns from these discussions that diction is a form of action (the action of the mouth that pronounces and enunciates sounds clearly) and that such form of action is equally susceptible to the conditions of proper use, or right action, as everything else. Aristotle's instructions thus begin with indivisible sounds—letters—that are arranged into compound sounds that give purpose to speech. Even barbarism has a place here, as he affirms when he states, "The corresponding use of strange words results in barbarism. A certain admixture, accordingly, of unfamiliar terms is necessary" (1458a30–32). The strange is necessary, Aristotle will go on to explain, because it helps counteract the monotony of the prosaic, all the while affording ordinary words a requisite clearness. Moreover, the strange is also the place of metaphor, which Aristotle famously posits as the greatest sign of genius (1459a7). The theory of muthos as the relation among part, place, and fit thus extends to diction, thereby establishing language itself as an original site of mimesis. By beginning with a correspondence between letter and sound and then affirming the right place of letters in the compound for the purposes of diction Aristotle provides an account of decorous sounds that will count as good speech. Diction, like poetry in general, cannot escape the necessity of proportion and fit as the overarching criteria of the good.

34. Rancière, *Mute Speech*, 97.

35. Rancière, *The Politics of Aesthetics*, 21–22.

36. Jacques Rancière, Rachel Bowlby, and Davide Panagia, "Ten Theses on Politics," *Theory and Event* 5, no. 3 (2001): thesis 7.

37. William E. Connolly, *A World of Becoming* (Durham, NC: Duke University Press, 2011), and *Capitalism and Christianity, American Style* (Durham, NC: Duke University Press, 2008), 67. Connolly's reliance on complexity theory enables him to distinguish between efficient and emergent causality and the political dynamics of these differing forms of connectivity. Rancière shares affinities with Connolly's specific concerns over the forms of connectivity that are treated exclusively as efficient causal structures, and, I would add, Rancière considers Aristotle's *Poetics* a forerunner of the police logic of efficient causality.

38. Jacques Rancière, *Film Fables* (London: Bloomsbury Academic, 2006), 1.

39. Jacques Rancière, *The Names of History: On the Poetics of Knowledge* (Minneapolis: University of Minnesota Press, 1994), 20.

40. Lisa Gitelman, *Paper Knowledge: Toward a Media History of Documents* (Durham,

NC: Duke University Press, 2014); John Guillory, "The Memo and Modernity," *Critical Inquiry* 31, no. 1 (2004): 108–32.

41. Davide Panagia and Jacques Rancière, "Dissenting Words: A Conversation with Jacques Rancière," *Diacritics* 30, no. 2 (2000): 115.

42. Ann M. Blair, *Too Much to Know: Managing Scholarly Information before the Modern Age* (New Haven, CT: Yale University Press, 2011), 11.

43. Rancière, *The Names of History*, 19.

44. Rancière, *The Names of History*, 38.

45. Rancière, *The Names of History*, 11.

46. Rancière, *The Names of History*, 61.

47. Rancière, *Film Fables*, 9.

48. Though not citing Rancière as a direct influence in her research, much of Libby Anker's articulation of the function of melodrama as the form of political discourse shares in this interrogation of an aesthetics of politics focused on formal plot structures, as when she writes, "Melodramatic discourses are so widespread, I argue, because they revive the guarantee of sovereign freedom for both the state and the individual in a neoliberal era when both seem out of reach." Elisabeth Robin Anker, *Orgies of Feeling: Melodrama and the Politics of Freedom* (Durham, NC: Duke University Press, 2014), 11.

49. In this we can sense Rancière extending Foucault's insights from *The Order of Things* regarding the historical shift from a classical to a modern episteme, as if part of his intellectual ambition is to address the questions Foucault raises in the first few pages of chapter 7 ("The Limits of Representation"): "Where did this unexpected mobility of epistemological arrangement suddenly come from, or the drift of positivities in relation to one another, or, deeper still, the alteration in their mode of being?" Michel Foucault, *The Order of Things: An Archaeology of the Human Sciences*, reissue ed. (New York: Vintage, 1994), 217.

50. Hassan Melehy, "Film Fables," in Jean-Philippe Deranty, *Jacques Rancière: Key Concepts* (New York: Routledge, 2014), 172.

51. Rancière, *Film Fables*, 2.

52. In the documentary film *Side by Side* (C. Kenneally, dir., 2012), this precise anxiety is championed as a reason why shooting with digital cameras as opposed to film is valuable. The director doesn't have to wait until the next day, once the film is developed, to view what has been shot and then decide or judge whether to keep the shot or shoot the scene again.

53. Rancière, *Film Fables*, 2.

54. François Truffaut, "A Certain Tendency of the French Cinema," in *Movies and Methods: An Anthology*, ed. Bill Nichols (Berkeley: University of California Press, 1976), 233.

55. Truffaut, "A Certain Tendency of the French Cinema," 229.

56. Truffaut, "A Certain Tendency of the French Cinema," 229.

57. Truffaut, "A Certain Tendency of the French Cinema," 232.

58. André Bazin, *What Is Cinema?* (Berkeley: University of California Press, 2005), 33–34.

59. Bazin, *What Is Cinema?*, 35.

60. Bazin, *What Is Cinema?*, 36.

61. Bazin, *What Is Cinema?*, 37, emphasis in original.

62. Sergei Eisenstein, *Film Form: Essays in Film Theory*, trans. Jay Leyda (New York: Harcourt, 1969), 81.

63. Daniel Morgan, "Rethinking Bazin: Ontology and Realist Aesthetics," *Critical Inquiry* 32, no. 3 (2006): 443–81.

64. Jean-Luc Godard, *Godard on Godard: Critical Writings by Jean-Luc Godard* (Cambridge, MA: Da Capo, 1986), 40. For those unfamiliar with the technical term, a moviola is a film editing machine.

65. Godard, *Godard on Godard*, 41.

66. Jacques Rancière, *The Intervals of Cinema* (London: Verso, 2014), 5.

67. Rancière, *The Intervals of Cinema*, 6.

68. Rancière, *The Names of History*, 33–34.

69. Walter Murch, *In the Blink of an Eye: A Perspective on Film Editing*, 2nd ed. (Los Angeles: Silman-James, 2001), 6.

70. Rancière, *Film Fables*, 171–87.

71. Rancière, *Film Fables*, 173.

72. Rancière, *The Intervals of Cinema*, 12.

73. Istvan Hont, *Jealousy of Trade: International Competition and the Nation-State in Historical Perspective* (Cambridge, MA: Harvard University Press, 2005), 11.

Chapter 3. Rancière's Style

1. Paul J. DiMaggio and Walter W. Powell, "The Iron Cage Revisited: Institutional Isomorphism and Collective Rationality in Organizational Fields," *American Sociological Review* 48, no. 2 (1983): 151.

2. Banu Bargu's political anthropology of death-fast struggles articulates a similar position that asks how it is that we might imagine a noninstrumentalist mode of political subjectivity whose agency is not reducible to preconceived accounts of successful action. See Banu Bargu, *Starve and Immolate: The Politics of Human Weapons* (New York: Columbia University Press, 2016).

3. Jacques Rancière, *Disagreement: Politics and Philosophy* (Minneapolis: University of Minnesota Press, 2004), 21.

4. I am grateful to my colleague Sarah Kareem for helping me formulate this insight.

5. Bruno Bosteels, "The Mexican Commune," in *Communism in the 21st Century*, ed. Shannon Brincat (Santa Barbara, CA: Greenwood, 2014), 132.

6. For a thorough treatment of Rancière's adoption of free indirect style, see James Swenson's "Style Indirect Libre" and especially his helpful definition of free indirect discourse as "a third-person narration of reported speech or thought, capable of smooth melding with exterior narration of actions and description of scenes, distinguished by the erasure of certain marking effects (quotation or other diacritical marks, 'he said that . . .' and so on)." In Gabriel Rockhill and Philip Watts, eds., *Jacques Rancière: History, Politics, Aesthetics* (Durham, NC: Duke University Press, 2009), 263.

7. Karl Marx, *Capital: A Critique of Political Economy* (London: Penguin, 2004), 139.

8. Jacques Rancière, *Aesthetics and Its Discontents* (Cambridge, UK: Polity, 2009), 14.

9. Jacques Rancière, Rachel Bowlby, and Davide Panagia, "Ten Theses on Politics," *Theory and Event* 5, no. 3 (2001): thesis 6.

10. Rancière, *Disagreement*, 115–16.

11. Within Anglo-American political theory, *disagreement* is an uncontested term of political discourse typically adaptable to a genre of political philosophy that wants to treat ethical problems as political — see Amy Gutmann and Dennis Thompson, *Democracy and Disagreement* (Cambridge, MA: Harvard University Press, 1998) — something that Rancière (*Aesthetics and Its Discontents*, 109–32) explicitly rejects. If pressed, and if the sense of disagreement must be kept, I would consider the term *disagreeable* more apt for Rancière's sense of "mésentente."

12. Consider Gilles Deleuze's claim that "the most general form of representation is thus

found in the element of a common sense understood as an upright nature and a good will." Gilles Deleuze, *Difference and Repetition*, trans. Paul Patton (New York: Columbia University Press, 1995), 131.

13. Jacques Rancière, *The Future of the Image*, trans. Gregory Elliott, reprint ed. (London: Verso, 2009), 34–43.

14. Pierre Bourdieu, *The Rules of Art: Genesis and Structure of the Literary Field* (Stanford, CA: Stanford University Press, 1996), 110.

15. Jacques Rancière, *Politics of Literature* (Cambridge, UK: Polity, 2011), 7.

16. Frances Ferguson, *Pornography, the Theory: What Utilitarianism Did to Action* (Chicago: University of Chicago Press, 2004), 101.

17. It is also noteworthy that this perpetual dynamic between reflective and determinative judgment that marks the iterative moment of criticism structures Rancière's own account of the dynamic relation between politics and the police, where every eruption of politics and every new partition of the sensible organize and potentiate a new possible police order. Hence the impossibility for Rancière of politics being something that can be sustained through time and the commitment to politics as an incipient force, or, as Jason Frank has explored it, as a "constituent moment." Jason Frank, *Constituent Moments: Enacting the People in Postrevolutionary America* (Durham, NC: Duke University Press, 2009). In this regard see Jonathan Havercroft and David Owen's discussion of "Rancière's example of soul-dawning of Menenius in relation to the plebs" and how the plebs "constitute themselves as an exemplar of *an-other* police order[;] they make *actual* another police order." Jonathan Havercroft and David Owen, "Soul-Blindness, Police Orders and Black Lives Matter: Wittgenstein, Cavell, and Rancière," *Political Theory*, July 11, 2016, 10.

18. To recall, the passage cited in the preface is the following: "The critic is the person who doesn't say what the work of art should be, or what the work of art is. The critic is the person who identifies what's happening." Jacques Rancière, *The Method of Equality: Interviews with Laurent Jeanpierre and Dork Zabunyan* (Hoboken, NJ: John Wiley and Sons, 2016), 65.

19. Thank you once again to Sarah Kareem for this helpful formulation.

20. Ronald Dworkin, "Law as Interpretation," *Critical Inquiry* 9, no. 1 (1982): 179–200.

21. Stanley Fish, "Working on the Chain Gang: Interpretation in the Law and in Literary Criticism," *Critical Inquiry* 9, no. 1 (1982): 201–16.

22. Rancière, *Politics of Literature*, 4.

23. Rancière, *Politics of Literature*, 10.

24. Rancière, *Politics of Literature*, 8.

25. Rancière, *Politics of Literature*, 7.

26. Rancière, *Politics of Literature*, 10.

27. Rey Chow, *Entanglements, or Transmedial Thinking about Capture* (Durham, NC: Duke University Press, 2012), 35. The Rancière essay to which Chow refers is "Why Emma Bovary Had to Be Killed," *Critical Inquiry* 34 (Winter 2008): 233–48 and appears as "The Putting to Death of Emma Bovary: Literature, Democracy, and Medicine," in *The Politics of Literature*. I cite from the latter version.

28. Chow, *Entanglements, or Transmedial Thinking about Capture*, 36.

29. Lauren Berlant, *Cruel Optimism* (Durham, NC: Duke University Press, 2011), 26.

30. Rancière, *Politics of Literature*, 54.

31. Sharon Cameron, *Impersonality: Seven Essays* (Chicago: University of Chicago Press, 2009), ix.

32. Rancière, *Politics of Literature*, 56, 60.

33. On Rancière and aesthetic disinterest, see Davide Panagia, *The Political Life of Sensation* (Durham, NC: Duke University Press, 2009).

34. It is Rancière's relation to arche that makes it so tempting to qualify his prose and his ideas as anarchic. And yet he neither prescribes nor endorses anarchism. Rather he submits the sense that democracy regards the absence of a priori (and hence necessary) qualifications for belonging and rule: "Democracy is the specific situation in which there is an absence of qualifications that, in turn, becomes the qualification for the exercise of a democratic *arche*" (Rancière et al., "Ten Theses on Politics," thesis 3). It is also tempting when reading such naked statements to collect Rancière's prose into a situationist imaginary. And though there might be many sensibilities in his ideas that solicit aspects of situationism, we must keep in mind two necessary qualifications of that movement: the moral theory of the image, which Rancière rejects prima facie; and the absence in Rancière of a prescription of the nature of situations for the production of specific effects (i.e., the absence of a causal principle that is necessary to situationist prescriptions).

35. Jacques Rancière, *Mute Speech: Literature, Critical Theory, and Politics* (New York: Columbia University Press, 2011), 122.

36. Jacques Rancière, *The Politics of Aesthetics* (New York: Continuum, 2004), 14.

37. Rancière, *Mute Speech*, 117.

38. Bruno Latour and Peter Weibel, *Making Things Public: Atmospheres of Democracy*, exhibition (Karlsruhe: ZKM/Center for Art and Media, 2005), 14.

39. Sheldon S. Wolin, "Political Theory as a Vocation," *American Political Science Review* 63, no. 4 (1969): 1075; Isabelle Stengers, "Including Non-Humans in Political Theory: Opening Pandora's Box?," in *Political Matter: Technoscience, Democracy, and Public Life*, ed. Bruce Baum and Sarah Whatmore (Minneapolis: University of Minnesota Press, 2010), 14.

40. For an adoption of Rancière's formalism see Caroline Levine's *Forms: Whole, Rhythm, Hierarchy, Network* (Princeton, NJ: Princeton University Press, 2015).

Chapter 4. Rancière's Democratic Realism

1. Here I paraphrase Frances Ferguson's account of Rancière's project in "Now It's Personal: D. A. Miller and Too-Close Reading," *Critical Inquiry* 41, no. 3 (2015): 263.

2. Jacques Rancière, *Aesthetics and Its Discontents* (Cambridge, UK: Polity, 2009), 21.

3. Jacques Rancière, *Film Fables* (London: Bloomsbury Academic, 2006), 149.

4. Jacques Rancière, *Aisthesis: Scenes from the Aesthetic Regime of Art*, trans. Zakir Paul (London: Verso, 2013), xv. *Farniente* is Italian for "do nothing" and is typically used to deride someone who is lazy and does not work or whose existence is pointless because whatever it is he or she may do, that doing is useless. The best English translation might be "pastime." That said, within the history of political thought, the farniente of leisure extends back to Aristotle's account of the place of leisure in political rule in the *Politics* (see esp. book 8). But it is also the temporality of the labor strike when workers take time to not work, or do nothing.

5. Jacques Rancière, Rachel Bowlby, and Davide Panagia, "Ten Theses on Politics," *Theory and Event* 5, no. 3 (2001): thesis 5.

6. Raymond Geuss, *Philosophy and Real Politics* (Princeton, NJ: Princeton University Press, 2008), 9.

7. Michel de Certeau, *The Writing of History* (New York: Columbia University Press, 1988), 42.

8. For a discussion of Rancière on aesthetic disinterest, see Davide Panagia, *The Political Life of Sensation* (Durham, NC: Duke University Press, 2010), 21–44.

9. Jacques Rancière, *Disagreement: Politics and Philosophy* (Minneapolis: University of Minnesota Press, 2004), xii.

10. Rancière, *Aisthesis*, 95.

11. Rancière, *Aisthesis*, 95.

12. Rancière, *Aisthesis*, 95.

13. Jacques Rancière, *The Politics of Aesthetics* (New York: Continuum, 2004), 14.

14. Jacques Rancière, "The Thread of the Novel," *Novel* 47, no. 2 (2014): 204.

15. Rancière, *Film Fables*, 172.

16. Jacques Rancière, *The Philosopher and His Poor*, ed. Andrew Parker, trans. Corinne Oster and John Drury (Durham, NC: Duke University Press, 2004), 44.

17. Rancière, *The Philosopher and His Poor*, 151.

18. Jacques Rancière, *The Emancipated Spectator* (London: Verso, 2014), 19.

19. Jacques Rancière, *Proletarian Nights: The Workers' Dream in Nineteenth-Century France* (London: Verso, 2014), xi.

20. Miriam Bratu Hansen, *Cinema and Experience: Siegfried Kracauer, Walter Benjamin, and Theodor W. Adorno*, ed. Edward Dimendberg (Berkeley: University of California Press, 2011), 36.

21. Georges Bataille, *The Accursed Share: An Essay on General Economy* (Cambridge, MA: Zone, 1991).

22. Rancière, *Aisthesis*, xv.

23. Consider, in this regard, Rancière's treatment of paratactic syntax as synonymous with montage in Jacques Rancière, *The Future of the Image*, trans. Gregory Elliott, reprint ed. (New York: Verso, 2009), 43–51.

24. Rancière, *Aisthesis*, 48.

25. Rancière, *Aisthesis*, 246–47.

26. Rancière, *Aisthesis*, 247.

27. Rancière, *Aisthesis*, 248.

28. Rancière, *Aisthesis*, 251.

29. See Theo Davis's *Ornamental Aesthetics: The Poetry of Attending in Thoreau, Dickinson, and Whitman* (Oxford: Oxford University Press, 2016) and her sense of the ornamentation as "an aesthetics in the sense of ways to attend, relate, and respond to the world" (3).

30. See Michel Foucault, "Governmentality" in Michel Foucault, Graham Burchell, Colin Gordon, and Peter Miller, *The Foucault Effect: Studies in Governmentality* (Chicago: University of Chicago Press, 1991), 251.

31. Rancière, *Aisthesis*, 228.

32. Rancière, *Aisthesis*, 228.

Conclusion

1. Giorgio Agamben, *Homo Sacer: Sovereign Power and Bare Life* (Stanford, CA: Stanford University Press, 1998); Giorgio Agamben, *State of Exception* (Chicago: University of Chicago Press, 2005); Carl Schmitt, *Political Theology: Four Chapters on the Concept of Sovereignty* (Chicago: University of Chicago Press, 2010).

2. Roger Caillois and Meyer Barash, *Man, Play, and Games* (Urbana: University of Illinois Press, 1961), 13.

3. This is a gesture that also finds expression in Jason Frank's felicitous encouragement to "attend to the nuances of these small dramas of self-authorization." Frank's sensorial redistribution of a postrevolutionary America is taken by the exemplarity of Rancière's scenographies, and for good reason: the constituent moments he makes manifest put on display the demos as both imminent to and emergent from the particularity of the scenes themselves; the demos is enacted and self-authorized. It partakes in its own constituency. Jason Frank, *Constituent Moments: Enacting the People in Postrevolutionary America* (Durham, NC: Duke University Press, 2009), 33.

4. Here I am reminded of Cristina Beltrán's discussion of immigrant action and her appeal to consider a larger and more complex emotive and political terrain characterized by what she identifies as "festive anger" that "involves [a] complex (and interconnected) set of civic emotions, including indignation, determination, irony, outrage, and joy." Thus she renders explicit that "while the marchers were hardly the hostile, anti-American presence that some anti-immigrant advocates claimed, neither were they the merry and non-threatening presence that liberal advocates and sympathizers depicted." The point in my raising this reminiscence is that the kind of politics Rancière and Beltrán imagine is one beyond the simple oppositions of threatening/familiar, unity/division. Indeed it is a politics that complicates the dividing line between those distinctions, a politics of indistinction. Cristina Beltrán, *The Trouble with Unity: Latino Politics and the Creation of Identity* (New York: Oxford University Press, 2010), 143.

5. In fact, he says exactly that in the *prelude* to the book: "One could consider these episodes, if so inclined, as a counter-history of 'artistic-modernity.'" Jacques Rancière, *Aisthesis: Scenes from the Aesthetic Regime of Art*, trans. Zakir Paul (London: Verso, 2013), XIII.

6. Jacques Rancière, *The Emancipated Spectator* (London: Verso, 2014), 46–47.

7. Inasmuch as he himself distinguishes his position regarding the relationship between art and criticism from that of Clement Greenberg, one would also have to distinguish his position from the ambition of Michael Fried to define an art object worthy of the name "art." Michael Fried, *Art and Objecthood: Essays and Reviews* (Chicago: University of Chicago Press, 1998), 148–72. That said, there are also many points of connection and shared

sensibilities between Fried's and Rancière's modernism worth exploring, though doing so is beyond the scope of the current project.

8. Jacques Rancière, *The Names of History: On the Poetics of Knowledge* (Minneapolis: University of Minnesota Press, 1994), 24.

9. Rancière, *The Names of History*, 25.

BIBLIOGRAPHY

Agamben, Giorgio. *Homo Sacer: Sovereign Power and Bare Life*. Stanford, CA: Stanford University Press, 1998.

————. *State of Exception*. Chicago: University of Chicago Press, 2005.

Althusser, Louis. *For Marx*. Translated by Ben Brewster. London: Verso, 2006.

————. *Lenin and Philosophy, and Other Essays*. New York: Monthly Review Press, 1971.

Anderson, Amanda. *The Way We Argue Now: A Study in the Cultures of Theory*. Princeton, NJ: Princeton University Press, 2005.

Anker, Elisabeth Robin. *Orgies of Feeling: Melodrama and the Politics of Freedom*. Durham, NC: Duke University Press, 2014.

Arendt, Hannah, and Ronald Beiner. *Lectures on Kant's Political Philosophy*. Chicago: University of Chicago Press, 1989.

Aristotle. *Metaphysics*. In *The Basic Works of Aristotle*. New York: Random House, 2009.

————. *Poetics*. In *The Basic Works of Aristotle*. New York: Random House, 2009.

Bargu, Banu. *Starve and Immolate: The Politics of Human Weapons*. New York: Columbia University Press, 2016.

Barthes, Roland. *Image-Music-Text*. New York: Macmillan, 1978.

Bataille, Georges. *The Accursed Share: An Essay on General Economy*. Cambridge, MA: Zone Books, 1991.

Bazin, André. *What Is Cinema?* Berkeley: University of California Press, 2005.

Beiner, Ronald. *Political Judgment*. London: Methuen, 1983.

Beltrán, Cristina. *The Trouble with Unity: Latino Politics and the Creation of Identity*. New York: Oxford University Press, 2010.

Bennett, Jane. *Vibrant Matter: A Political Ecology of Things*. Durham, NC: Duke University Press, 2009.

Berlant, Lauren. *Cruel Optimism*. Durham, NC: Duke University Press, 2011.

Bingham, Charles, and Gert Biesta. *Jacques Rancière: Education, Truth, Emancipation*. New York: A&C Black, 2010.

Blair, Ann M. *Too Much to Know: Managing Scholarly Information before the Modern Age*. New Haven, CT: Yale University Press, 2011.

Bolter, J. David, and Richard A. Grusin. *Remediation: Understanding New Media*. Cambridge, MA: MIT Press, 2000.

Bosteels, Bruno. "The Mexican Commune." In *Communism in the 21st Century*, edited by Shannon Brincat. Santa Barbara, CA: Greenwood, 2014.

Bourdieu, Pierre. *Distinction: A Social Critique of the Judgement of Taste*. Cambridge, MA: Harvard University Press, 1984.

———. *The Rules of Art: Genesis and Structure of the Literary Field*. Stanford, CA: Stanford University Press, 1996.

Briault, Thierry, and Jacques Rancière. "Entretien avec Jacques Rancière sur la Plastique et le Sens Commun." *Club de Mediapart*, November 25, 2015. https://blogs.mediapart.fr/thierry-briault/blog/251115/entretien-avec-jacques-ranciere-sur-la-plastique-et-le-sens-commun.

Brossat, Alain. "La notion de dispositif chez Michel Foucault." In *Miroir, appareils et autres dispositifs*, edited by Soko Phay-Vakalis. Paris: Editions l'Harmattan, 2009.

Caillois, Roger, and Meyer Barash. *Man, Play, and Games*. Urbana: University of Illinois Press, 1961.

Cameron, Sharon. *Impersonality: Seven Essays*. Chicago: University of Chicago Press, 2009.

Chambers, Samuel A. *The Lessons of Rancière*. Oxford: Oxford University Press, 2014.

Chandler, James. *An Archaeology of Sympathy: The Sentimental Mode in Literature and Cinema*. Chicago: University of Chicago Press, 2013.

Chari, Anita. *A Political Economy of the Senses: Neoliberalism, Reification, Critique*. New York: Columbia University Press, 2015.

Chow, Rey. *Entanglements, or Transmedial Thinking about Capture*. Durham, NC: Duke University Press, 2012.

Chwe, Michael Suk-Young. *Rational Ritual: Culture, Coordination, and Common Knowledge*. Princeton, NJ: Princeton University Press, 2003.

Connolly, William E. *Capitalism and Christianity, American Style*. Durham, NC: Duke University Press, 2008.

———. *The Ethos of Pluralization*. Minneapolis: University of Minnesota Press, 1995.

———. *A World of Becoming*. Durham, NC: Duke University Press, 2011.

Danto, Arthur Coleman. *The Transfiguration of the Commonplace: A Philosophy of Art*. Cambridge, MA: Harvard University Press, 1981.

Davis, Oliver. *Jacques Rancière*. Hoboken, NJ: John Wiley, 2013.

———. *Rancière Now*. Cambridge, UK: Polity, 2013.

Davis, Oliver, and Jacques Rancière. "On Aisthesis: An Interview." In *Ranciere Now*, by Oliver Davis. Cambridge, UK: Polity, 2013.

Davis, Theo. *Ornamental Aesthetics: The Poetry of Attending in Thoreau, Dickinson, and Whitman*. Oxford: Oxford University Press, 2016.

de Certeau, Michel. *The Writing of History*. New York: Columbia University Press, 1988.

Deleuze, Gilles. *Difference and Repetition*. Translated by Paul Patton. New York: Columbia University Press, 1995.

Deranty, Jean-Philippe. *Jacques Rancière: Key Concepts*. New York: Routledge, 2014.

Derrida, Jacques. "White Mythology." In *Margins of Philosophy*. Chicago: University of Chicago Press, 1982.

DiMaggio, Paul J., and Walter W. Powell. "The Iron Cage Revisited: Institutional Isomorphism and Collective Rationality in Organizational Fields." *American Sociological Review* 48, no. 2 (1983): 147–60. doi:10.2307/2095101.

Dworkin, Ronald. "Law as Interpretation." *Critical Inquiry* 9, no. 1 (1982): 179–200.

Eagleton, Terry. *The Ideology of the Aesthetic*. Hoboken, NJ: Wiley, 1991.

Eisenstein, Sergei. *Film Form: Essays in Film Theory*. Translated by Jay Leyda. New York: Harcourt, 1969.

Ferguson, Frances. "Jane Austen, *Emma*, and the Impact of Form." MLQ: *Modern Language Quarterly* 61, no. 1 (2000): 157–80.

———. "Now It's Personal: D. A. Miller and Too-Close Reading." *Critical Inquiry* 41, no. 3 (2015): 521–40. doi:10.1086/680084.

———. "Our I. A. Richards Moment: The Machine and Its Adjustments." In *Theory Aside*, edited by Jason Potts and Daniel Stout. Durham, NC: Duke University Press, 2014.

———. *Pornography, the Theory: What Utilitarianism Did to Action*. Chicago: University of Chicago Press, 2004.

Ferguson, Kennan. *The Politics of Judgment: Aesthetics, Identity, and Political Theory*. Lanham, MD: Lexington Books, 2007.

Ferry, Luc, and Alain Renaut. *French Philosophy of the Sixties: An Essay on Antihumanism*. Amherst: University of Massachusetts Press, 1990.

Fish, Stanley. "Working on the Chain Gang: Interpretation in the Law and in Literary Criticism." *Critical Inquiry* 9, no. 1 (1982): 201–16.

Foucault, Michel. *The Foucault Reader*. New York: Pantheon, 1984.

———. *The Order of Things: An Archaeology of the Human Sciences*. Reissue ed. New York: Vintage, 1994.

Foucault, Michel, Graham Burchell, Colin Gordon, and Peter Miller. *The Foucault Effect: Studies in Governmentality*. Chicago: University of Chicago Press, 1991.

Frank, Jason. *Constituent Moments: Enacting the People in Postrevolutionary America*. Durham, NC: Duke University Press, 2009.

———. "Logical Revolts: Jacques Rancière and Political Subjectivization." *Political Theory* 43, no. 2 (2015): 249–61.

Freeden, Michael. *Ideologies and Political Theory: A Conceptual Approach*. Oxford: Clarendon, 1998.

Fried, Michael. *Art and Objecthood: Essays and Reviews*. Chicago: University of Chicago Press, 1998.

Geuss, Raymond. *Philosophy and Real Politics*. Princeton, NJ: Princeton University Press, 2008.

Gitelman, Lisa. *Paper Knowledge: Toward a Media History of Documents*. Durham, NC: Duke University Press, 2014.

Godard, Jean-Luc, dir. *Bande à part*. 1964.

———. *A bout de souffle*. 1960.

———. *Godard on Godard: Critical Writings by Jean-Luc Godard*. Cambridge, MA: Da Capo, 1986.

———. *Histoire(s) du cinéma*. TV mini-series. 1989–1999.

Grusin, Richard. "Radical Mediation." *Critical Inquiry* 42, no. 1 (2015): 124–48.

Guillory, John. "How Scholars Read." *ADE Bulletin*, no. 146 (Fall 2008): 8–17.

———. "The Memo and Modernity." *Critical Inquiry* 31, no. 1 (2004): 108–32. doi:10.1086/427304.

Gutmann, Amy, and Dennis F. Thompson. *Democracy and Disagreement*. Cambridge, MA: Harvard University Press, 1998.

Habermas, Jürgen. *The Philosophical Discourse of Modernity: Twelve Lectures*. Translated by Frederick G. Lawrence. Reprint ed. Cambridge, MA: MIT Press, 1990.

Halliwell, Stephen. *Aristotle's Poetics*. Chicago: University of Chicago Press, 1986.

Hallward, Peter. "Staging Equality." *New Left Review* 2, no. 37 (2006): 109–29.

Hansen, Miriam Bratu. *Cinema and Experience: Siegfried Kracauer, Walter Benjamin, and Theodor W. Adorno*. Edited by Edward Dimendberg. Berkeley: University of California Press, 2011.

Hariman, Robert. *Political Style: The Artistry of Power*. Chicago: University of Chicago Press, 2010.

Havercroft, Jonathan, and David Owen. "Soul-Blindness, Police Orders and Black Lives Matter: Wittgenstein, Cavell, and Rancière." *Political Theory*, July 11, 2016. doi:10.1177/0090591716657857.

Heidegger, Martin. *Being and Time*. New York: HarperCollins, 2008.

Honig, Bonnie. *Antigone, Interrupted*. Cambridge: Cambridge University Press, 2013.

———. *Democracy and the Foreigner*. Princeton, NJ: Princeton University Press, 2001.

Hont, Istvan. *Jealousy of Trade: International Competition and the Nation-State in Historical Perspective*. Cambridge, MA: Harvard University Press, 2005.

Jameson, Fredric. *The Political Unconscious: Narrative as a Socially Symbolic Act*. Ithaca, NY: Cornell University Press, 1991.

Jay, Martin. "'The Aesthetic Ideology' as Ideology; or, What Does It Mean to Aestheticize Politics?" *Cultural Critique*, no. 21 (1992): 41–61. doi:10.2307/1354116.

Koopman, Colin. *Genealogy as Critique: Foucault and the Problems of Modernity*. Bloomington: Indiana University Press, 2013.

Krause, Sharon R. *Freedom beyond Sovereignty: Reconstructing Liberal Individualism*. Chicago: University of Chicago Press, 2015.

Krieger, Murray. *Ekphrasis: The Illusion of the Natural Sign*. Baltimore: Johns Hopkins University Press, 1992.

Kuhn, Thomas S. *The Structure of Scientific Revolutions: 50th Anniversary Edition*. Chicago: University of Chicago Press, 2012.

Latour, Bruno, and Peter Weibel. *Making Things Public: Atmospheres of Democracy*. Exhibition. Karlsruhe: ZKM/Center for Art and Media, 2005.

Levine, Caroline. *Forms: Whole, Rhythm, Hierarchy, Network*. Princeton, NJ: Princeton University Press, 2015.

Levy, Jacob T. *Rationalism, Pluralism, and Freedom*. New York: Oxford University Press, 2015.

Lévy, Jacques, Juliette Rennes, and David Zerbib. "Jacques Rancière: 'Les territoires de la pensée partagée.'" *Revue électronique des sciences humaines et sociales*, January 8, 2007. http://www.espacestemps.net/articles/jacques-ranciere-les-territoires-de -la-pensee-partagee/.

Lewis, Charlton T., and Charles Short, eds. *A Latin Dictionary*. Perseus Digital Library. Accessed April 15, 2016. http://www.perseus.tufts.edu/hopper/text?doc=Perseus% 3Atext%3A1999.04.0059%3Aentry%3Ddecorus.

Lima, Manuel. *Visual Complexity: Mapping Patterns of Information*. Reprint ed. New York: Princeton Architectural Press, 2013.

Macpherson, Sandra. "A Little Formalism." ELH 82, no. 2 (2015): 385–405. doi:10.1353/ elh.2015.0025.

Martel, James. *Textual Conspiracies: Walter Benjamin, Idolatry, and Political Theory*. Ann Arbor: University of Michigan Press, 2011.

Marx, Karl. *Capital: A Critique of Political Economy*. London: Penguin, 2004.

Massumi, Brian. *Politics of Affect*. Hoboken, NJ: John Wiley and Sons, 2015.

May, Todd. *Contemporary Political Movements and the Thought of Jacques Rancière: Equality in Action*. Edinburgh: Edinburgh University Press, 2010.

———. *The Political Thought of Jacques Rancière: Creating Equality*. Edinburgh: Edinburgh University Press, 2008.

Menely, Tobias. *The Animal Claim: Sensibility and the Creaturely Voice*. Chicago: University of Chicago Press, 2015.

Morgan, Daniel. "Rethinking Bazin: Ontology and Realist Aesthetics." *Critical Inquiry* 32, no. 3 (2006): 443–81. doi:10.1086/505375.

Murch, Walter. *In the Blink of an Eye: A Perspective on Film Editing*. 2nd ed. Los Angeles: Silman-James, 2001.

Nazar, Hina. *Enlightened Sentiments: Judgment and Autonomy in the Age of Sensibility*. New York: Fordham University Press, 2012.

Norval, Aletta J. "'Writing a Name in the Sky': Rancière, Cavell, and the Possibility of Egalitarian Inscription." *American Political Science Review* 106, no. 4 (2012): 810–26. doi:10.1017/S0003055412000445.

Nussbaum, Martha C. *Love's Knowledge: Essays on Philosophy and Literature*. New York: Oxford University Press, 1992.

Pagden, Anthony. *The Enlightenment: And Why It Still Matters*. New York: Random House, 2013.

Panagia, Davide. *The Political Life of Sensation*. Durham, NC: Duke University Press, 2009.

———. *Ten Theses for an Aesthetics of Politics*. Forerunners: Ideas First. Minneapolis: University of Minnesota Press, 2016.

————. "A Theory of Aspects: Media Participation and Political Theory." *New Literary History* 45, no. 4 (2014): 527–48.

Panagia, Davide, and Jacques Rancière. "Dissenting Words: A Conversation with Jacques Rancière." *Diacritics* 30, no. 2 (2000): 113–26.

Rancière, Jacques. *Aesthetics and Its Discontents*. Cambridge, UK: Polity, 2009.

————. *Aisthesis: Scenes from the Aesthetic Regime of Art*. Translated by Zakir Paul. London: Verso, 2013.

————. *Althusser's Lesson*. London: Bloomsbury, 2011.

————. *Disagreement: Politics and Philosophy*. Minneapolis: University of Minnesota Press, 2004.

————. *The Emancipated Spectator*. London: Verso, 2014.

————. *Film Fables*. London: Bloomsbury Academic, 2006.

————. *The Future of the Image*. Translated by Gregory Elliott. Reprint ed. London: Verso, 2009.

————. *The Ignorant Schoolmaster: Five Lessons in Intellectual Emancipation*. Stanford, CA: Stanford University Press, 1991.

————. *The Intellectual and His People: Staging the People*. Vol. 2. London: Verso, 2012.

————. *The Intervals of Cinema*. London: Verso, 2014.

————. *La leçon d'Althusser*. Paris: Gallimard, 1975.

————. *The Method of Equality: Interviews with Laurent Jeanpierre and Dork Zabunyan*. Hoboken, NJ: John Wiley and Sons, 2016.

————. *Mute Speech: Literature, Critical Theory, and Politics*. New York: Columbia University Press, 2011.

————. *The Names of History: On the Poetics of Knowledge*. Minneapolis: University of Minnesota Press, 1994.

————. *The Philosopher and His Poor*. Edited by Andrew Parker. Translated by Corinne Oster and John Drury. Durham, NC: Duke University Press, 2004.

————. "Politics, Identification, and Subjectivization." *October* 61 (1992): 58–64.

————. *The Politics of Aesthetics*. New York: Continuum, 2004.

————. *Politics of Literature*. Cambridge, UK: Polity, 2011.

————. *Proletarian Nights: The Workers' Dream in Nineteenth-Century France*. London: Verso, 2014.

————. *Staging the People: The Proletarian and His Double*. Translated by David Fernbach. London: Verso, 2011.

————. "The Thread of the Novel." *Novel* 47, no. 2 (2014): 196–209. doi:10.1215/00295132-2647149.

Rancière, Jacques, Rachel Bowlby, and Davide Panagia. "Ten Theses on Politics." *Theory and Event* 5, no. 3 (2001). doi:10.1353/tae.2001.0028.

Rancière, Jacques, Fulvia Carnevale, and John Kelsey. "Art of the Possible: Fulvia Carnevale and John Kelsey in Conversation with Jacques Rancière." *Artforum* 45, no. 7 (2007): 256–69.

Renault, Emmanuel. "The Many Marx of Jacques Rancière." In *Jacques Ranciere and the*

Contemporary Scene: The Philosophy of Radical Equality, edited by Jean-Philippe Deranty and Alison Ross. New York: A&C Black, 2012.

Ricoeur, Paul. *The Rule of Metaphor: Multi-Disciplinary Studies of the Creation of Meaning in Language*. Toronto: University of Toronto Press, 1981.

————. *Time and Narrative*. Vol. 1. Translated by Kathleen McLaughlin and David Pellauer. Chicago: University of Chicago Press, 1990.

Ricoeur, Paul, and John B. Thompson. *Hermeneutics and the Human Sciences: Essays on Language, Action and Interpretation*. Cambridge: Cambridge University Press, 1981.

Rifkin, Adrian. "Cultural Movement and the Paris Commune." *Art History* 2, no. 2 (1979): 201–20. doi:10.1111/j.1467-8365.1979.tb00042.x.

Rockhill, Gabriel, and Philip Watts, eds. *Jacques Rancière: History, Politics, Aesthetics*. Durham, NC: Duke University Press, 2009.

Rogers, Melvin. "Race and Republicanism: Early African American Political Thought." *La Revue internationale de philosophie*. Forthcoming.

Ross, Kristin. *Communal Luxury: The Political Imaginary of the Paris Commune*. London: Verso, 2015.

————. *May '68 and Its Afterlives*. Chicago: University of Chicago Press, 2004.

Rousseau, Jean-Jacques. *Rousseau: "The Discourses" and Other Early Political Writings*. Edited by Victor Gourevitch. Cambridge: Cambridge University Press, 1997.

Schmitt, Carl. *Political Theology: Four Chapters on the Concept of Sovereignty*. Chicago: University of Chicago Press, 2010.

Shapiro, Michael J. *Studies in Trans-Disciplinary Method: After the Aesthetic Turn*. New York: Routledge, 2013.

Skinner, Quentin. "Meaning and Understanding in the History of Ideas." In *Meaning and Context: Quentin Skinner and His Critics*, edited by James Tully. Cambridge, UK: Polity, 1988.

Stengers, Isabelle. "Including Non-Humans in Political Theory: Opening Pandora's Box?" In *Political Matter: Technoscience, Democracy, and Public Life*, edited by Bruce Baum and Sarah Whatmore. Minneapolis: University of Minnesota Press, 2010.

Sterne, Jonathan. *MP3: The Meaning of a Format*. Durham, NC: Duke University Press, 2012.

Struever, Nancy S. *The Language of History in the Renaissance: Rhetoric and Historical Consciousness in Florentine Humanism*. Princeton, NJ: Princeton University Press, 2015.

Tanke, Joseph J. *Jacques Rancière: An Introduction*. New York: A&C Black, 2011.

Tausk, Victor. "On the Origin of the 'Influence Machine' in Schizophrenia." *Journal of Psychotherapy Practice and Research* 1, no. 2 (1992): 185–206.

Taylor, Charles. "Interpretations and the Sciences of Man." In *Philosophical Papers*. Vol. 2, *Philosophy and the Human Sciences*. Cambridge: Cambridge University Press, 1985.

Tormey, Simon. *The End of Representative Politics*. Hoboken, NJ: John Wiley and Sons, 2015.

Truffaut, François. "A Certain Tendency of the French Cinema." In *Movies and Meth-*

ods: An Anthology, edited by Bill Nichols. Berkeley: University of California Press, 1976.

Tully, James. *On Global Citizenship: James Tully in Dialogue.* London: Bloomsbury Academic, 2014.

———. *Public Philosophy in a New Key.* Vol. 1, *Democracy and Civic Freedom.* Cambridge: Cambridge University Press, 2008.

Wittgenstein, Ludwig. *Philosophical Investigations.* 3rd ed. New York: Pearson, 1973.

Wolin, Sheldon S. "Political Theory as a Vocation." *American Political Science Review* 63, no. 4 (1969): 1062–82. doi:10.1017/S000305540026320X.

———. *Politics and Vision: Continuity and Innovation in Western Political Thought.* Princeton, NJ: Princeton University Press, 2009.

Young, Liam. "On Lists and Networks: An Archaeology of Form." *Amodern* 2: *Archaeology,* 2013. http://amodern.net/article/on-lists-and-networks/.

Zerilli, Linda M. G. *A Democratic Theory of Judgment.* Chicago: University of Chicago Press, 2016.

———. *Feminism and the Abyss of Freedom.* Chicago: University of Chicago Press, 2005.

do-nothing. *See farniente*

Dworkin, Ronald, 77

ecology, 37–38, 49. *See also* relationality

Eisenstein, Sergei, 59

ekphrasis, 19, 21–22, 30

emancipation, 2–4, 6–7, 9, 17, 24, 29–30, 85, 90–93

emergence, xi, xii, 101, 103

emplotment, 8–9, 13–14, 43–48, 51–52, 54–56, 58, 119n33

enclosure, 19–20. *See also* commons, the; private property

epistemic break, 11, 22, 24–26

Epstein, Jean, 51–52

equality, 2–4, 16, 29–30, 32, 80–81, 85, 89–91. *See also* politics

equivalence, 31, 58, 66–71, 83, 96

The Ethos of Pluralization (Connolly), 109n23

Evans, Walker, 94–97, 102–3

"The Evolution of the Language of Cinema" (Bazin), 59

farniente, 86, 92–93, 96–100, 125n4

Feminism and the Abyss of Freedom (Zerilli), x–xi

Ferguson, Frances, 6, 72–73, 78

Film Fables (Rancière), 43, 51, 64

Fish, Stanley, 77

fit(ting). *See* decorum

Flaubert, Gustave, 3, 18, 72–80, 83, 110n34

Foucault, Michel, 27–28, 110n34, 116n47, 120n49

Frank, Jason, 123n17, 127n3

Freeden, Michael, 38

free indirect discourse, 12, 17–18, 28, 34–35, 64–65, 72–79, 83–84, 86, 110n34. *See also style indirect libre*

Fried, Michael, 127n7

frivolousness, 96–97

Fuller, Loïe, 88

Geuss, Raymond, 86

Godard, Jean-Luc, 7–8, 44, 57–59, 61, 89, 91

Greenberg, Clement, 127n7

Grusin, Richard, 20–21

Guillory, John, 35, 116n48

Hallward, Peter, 4

Hansen, Miriam Bratu, 92

Hariman, Robert, 41–42

Havercroft, Jonathan, 15

Histoire(s) du cinema (Godard), 61

The History of Art (Winckelmann), 14

Hogarth, William, 88

Honig, Bonnie, 105n7, 115n44

Hume, David, 3, 23

Hutcheson, Francis, 3, 23

hylomorphism, 8, 17, 43–44, 46–47, 111n35

ideology, 24–25. *See also* Althusser, Louis

"Ideology and Ideological State Apparatuses" (Althusser), 24

ignorant gestu, xii, 6, 103

The Ignorant Schoolmaster (Rancière), 29

immanence, 6, 14–15, 84, 99–100, 102–3

impersonality, 79–82, 110n34. *See also* disinterest

impropriety, 6–9, 49, 53, 71–72, 85–88, 91–93, 95–97

in-betweenness, 22–23, 112n12. *See also partager*

indirection, 79–82. *See also style indirect libre*

indistinction, 6, 10–11, 19–21, 30–31, 80–82, 88, 90–91, 97, 101

intelligibility, xii, 10–11, 17–18, 31, 48–51, 68, 77, 87–91

interpellation, xii, 11, 24–25, 50. *See also* Althusser, Louis

The Intervals of Cinema (Rancière), 60